THE CRUSADES, CHRISTIANITY, AND ISLAM

The Bampton Lectures in America

The Prospects of Western Civilization, Arnold J. Toynbee 1940

New Discoveries in Medicine: Their Effect on the Public Health, Paul R. Hawley 1950

Gospel and Law: The Relation of Faith and Ethics in Early Christianity,
Charles H. Dodd 1951

Art and Technics, Lewis Mumford 1952; reprinted with a new introduction
by Casey Nelson Blake 2000

Modern Science and Modern Man, James B. Conant 1952

Challenges to Contemporary Medicine, Alan Gregg 1956

The Idea of Revelation in Recent Thought, John Baillie 1956

Four Steps Toward Modern Art: Giorgione, Caravaggio, Manet, Cezanne,
Lionello Venturi 1956

Science in the Making, Joel Henry Hildebrand 1957

Prescription for Survival, Brock Chisholm 1957

The Importance of Being Human: Some Aspects of the Christian Doctrine of Man,
Eric Lionel Mascall 1958

The Art of William Blake, Sir Anthony Frederick Blunt 1959

From Miasmas to Molecules, William Barry Wood 1961

Christianity and the Encounter of the World Religions, Paul Tillich 1963

A Natural Perspective: The Development of Shakespearean Comedy and Romance,
Northrop Frye 1965

Man in the Universe, Fred Hoyle 1966

Mental Illness: Progress and Prospects, Robert H. Felix 1967

The Religious Significance of Atheism, Alasdair MacIntyre and Paul Ricoeur 1969

Victorian Architecture: Four Studies in Evaluation, Sir John Summerson 1970

Magic, Science, and Civilization, Jacob Bronowski 1975

Titian: His World and His Legacy, David Rosand, ed. 1982

Faith and Reason, Anthony Kenny 1983

Language and Information, Zellig Harris 1988

The Painter's Practice: How Artists Lived and Worked in Traditional China,
James Cahill 1994

THE CRUSADES, CHRISTIANITY, AND ISLAM

Jonathan Riley-Smith

COLUMBIA UNIVERSITY PRESS   NEW YORK

COLUMBIA UNIVERSITY PRESS

Publishers Since 1893

NEW YORK   CHICHESTER, WEST SUSSEX

A Caravan book. For more information, visit www.caravanbooks.org

Library of Congress Cataloging-in-Publication Data

Riley-Smith, Jonathan Simon Christopher, 1938–

The crusades, Christianity, and Islam / Jonathan Riley-Smith.

p.   cm. — (Bampton lectures in America)

Includes bibliographical references and index.

ISBN 978-0-231-14624-1 (cloth : alk. paper) — ISBN 978-0-231-51794-2 (e-book)

1. Crusades.   2. Christianity and other religions.   3. Islam—Relations—Christianity.

I. Title.   II. Series.

D157.R536   2008

909.07—dc22   2008001201

Printed in the United States of America

c 10 9 8 7 6 5 4 3 2 1

CONTENTS

THE CRUSADES, CHRISTIANITY, AND ISLAM

INTRODUCTION

The First Crusade was fought between 1096 and 1102. The crusading movement was at its most popular from the late twelfth century to the late fourteenth, but was still active in the fifteenth and sixteenth centuries. The last crusade league was the Holy League, which began the recovery of the Balkans from the Turks between 1684 and 1699. The last operative order-state of a military order was Hospitaller Malta, which succumbed to Napoleon in 1798. A new military order was founded as late as 1890, although it had a very short life, as we will see. We are faced by a movement that lasted for hundreds of years and touched the lives of the ancestors of everyone today of Western European descent and of many of Eastern European, Jewish, and Muslim descent as well. No one can feel comfortable about this aspect of our collective experience, but for intellectual as well as moral reasons the role of its historians is an awkward one. In the last thirty years their understanding of the movement has led them to reject the long-held belief that it was defined solely by its theaters of operation in the Levant and its hostility toward Islam[1]—with the consequence that in their eyes the Muslims move slightly off center stage—and many of them have begun to face up to the ideas and motivation of the crusaders.[2] The more they do so the more they find themselves *contra mundum* or, at least, *contra mundum Christianum*, because their conception of the realities of crusading turns out to be in conflict with those of nearly everyone else, from leading churchmen and scholars in other fields to the general public.

In many ways the Crusades deserve their poor reputation. Like all religious wars, they were marked by indiscipline and atrocities. As military expeditions that were also pilgrimages, they had to be open to all, sinners as well as saints—especially sinners—and there was no system for screening volunteers to identify the unsuitable, who might include psychopaths. The popes, who authorized them, lost control once the armies were on the march, and the fact that the laymen who were entrusted with leadership in the field were volunteers made adequate chains of command hard to establish. The methods employed to encourage recruitment heightened emotions in men who could then be exposed to tension and alienation for very long periods of time. Although it is hard to draw lessons from modern combat psychiatry and apply them to situations hundreds of years ago, it is known that volunteers are more likely to commit atrocities than conscripts and that over-long exposure to stress is bad for efficiency and discipline.[3]

Measures assuring greater cohesion and control began to be adopted in the thirteenth century. The crusaders bound for the Levant were being transported by sea, which reduced the number of noncombatants, since the poor could not afford a maritime passage, and forced the planners to think about logistics, which were less problematic now that the armies were not encumbered by hordes of the unsuitable. The decision of the papacy to raise large sums from the taxation of the church, which were then allotted to those leaders who were taking the cross, provided a means of subsidizing crusaders through their commanders and therefore of making them more amenable,[4] while the introduction from the 1330s onward of crusade leagues enabled the states in these alliances to make use of their "regular" forces (if one can use that term), combining the benefits of crusading with more professional fighting elements.[5] A huge gulf separates the scratch forces of the twelfth century from the Christian navy, which fought the battle of Lepanto in 1571, or the armies of the Holy League, which were recovering Hungary in the 1680s.

There was obviously more to crusading in the central Middle Ages than cruelty and indiscipline, but nothing can eradicate from present-day minds the impression left by those unruly armies. Among the descendants of those who perceive themselves to have been damaged by them, the Muslims and the Greek Orthodox have developed mythistories—to use a word adopted by Dr. Gary Dickson in another context—in which memories of genuine injuries have been embroidered, even re-created, long after the events concerned.[6] The perception most modern Muslims have of the Crusades dates only from the end of the nineteenth century, as we shall see. It constituted, in fact, a transference onto the past of feelings of alienation engendered by imperialism. In the case of the Greeks it was the failure of the West to come to the assistance of the rump of the Byzantine empire in 1453—two and a half centuries after the sack of Constantinople by the Fourth Crusade—and resentment building up during the long years of subjection to the Ottomans that seem to have fanned the bitterness, although it is true that the Greek church had suffered from its refusal to reconcile itself with Latin Christianity on papal terms.

The modern reactions of the Jews, who have more right than the members of any other community to consider themselves to have been the innocent victims of the crusaders, are more complex. Pogroms marked the departure of many of the Crusades to the East in the central Middle Ages and the Jews, who memorialized their sufferings in the Ashkenazi liturgy,[7] have naturally been inclined to link them to the Holocaust of the 1940s through a chain of terrible events extending over eight and a half centuries.[8] In the last thirty years, however, a more focused approach has emerged among historians of the early persecutions,[9] while those Israelis who are interested in the settlements the crusaders established in the East treat them much more positively than they did in the past, demonstrating how strongly modern priorities are echoed in interpretations of history. The establishment of the state of Israel on much of the territory occupied by the "crusader" kingdom of Jerusalem has led to scholarly and popular engagement with the kingdom's history and institutions. These used to be compared very unfavorably with the achievements of modern Zionism, but they are now being portrayed in a better light. Even quite minor "crusader" sites in Israel are being developed as tourist centers, while Professor Ronnie Ellenblum has traced a progression

> from the "Jewish" reading of its history, focusing on the slaughter of the Rhineland Jewish communities in 1096, to a Zionist reading of the crusades, focusing on seeing them as an inverse prefiguration of the future Zionist movement, and finally to a reading of the crusades as part of my own country, and to a certain degree, as part of my own history.[10]

On the other hand, leading Christian churchmen in the Western tradition—Catholic and Protestant—are not only ashamed by the fact of the Crusades but are also in a state of self-denial. Embarrassed by this aspect of their past, they have underplayed its importance in their history, while maintaining that it really had very little to do with their religion. In a recent lecture the archbishop of Canterbury stated that "Most Christians would now say that . . . the crusades . . . were serious betrayals of many of the central beliefs of the Christian faith."[11] He was echoed by the professor of the History of the Church in Oxford, who asserted that the Crusades constituted "a bizarre centuries-long episode in which western Christianity wilfully ignored its Master's principles of love and forgiveness."[12] Pope John Paul II, who never apologized for the Crusades but gave the impression that he was doing so, would probably have agreed. The issue I have with these leading representatives of the consensus relates not to their theology but to their knowledge of history, because underlying their opinions is the belief that the crusading movement was an aberration, a departure from the norm in Christian history.

This is wish-fulfillment, stemming from a desire to reshape the past of one's religion into a more acceptable form. As recently as the seventeenth century, and perhaps more recently still, most Christians—Catholic, Orthodox, and Protestant—had in general no problem with the idea of holy war. From the twelfth century to the seventeenth the consensus of the teaching of the Catholic bishops was that qualified men had a moral obligation to take the cross. This was reinforced by the support of a succession of men and women generally recognized as saints: Bernard of Clairvaux, Dominic, Louis of France, Thomas Aquinas, Bridget of Sweden, Catherine of Siena, John of Capistrano, even probably Francis of Assisi.[13] From Urban II in 1095 to Innocent XI in 1684, pope after pope wrote, or authorized the dispatch of, letters in which the faithful were summoned to crusade, offered spiritual privileges if they responded and threatened with divine judgment if they did not, and the papacy recognized a new type of religious institute in approving of and privileging the military orders. At least six general councils of the church legislated for crusades and two of them, the Fourth Lateran Council (1215) and the Second Council of Lyons (1274), published the constitutions *Ad liberandam* and *Pro zelo fidei*, which were among the movement's defining documents.[14] The early Protestants' rejection of the papal *magisterium* and salvation through works did not prevent them preaching the right of Christians to take up arms in their own defense against the Turks, and it has been pointed out that Martin Luther's approach "resembled the Catholic crusade in a number of key respects, notably its emphasis on repentance and prayer."[15] The Huguenot captain Francis of La Noue wrote in the early 1580s a proposal for a modified crusade, without an indulgence, to recover Constantinople.[16]

It should also be remembered that no crusade could ever have left Europe merely because a pope had authorized it or a general council had issued some declaration concerning it. Crusaders were on the whole volunteers and this meant that the laity—the less well-off as well as kings and nobles; women as well as men—had to respond positively to an appeal from the leaders of the church before an army of any size could be mustered. Although the number of individuals taking the cross at any given time was always a tiny minority of those in Western Europe qualified to do so, they often had general, and sometimes enthusiastic, support from the rest of the populace. Western Christendom shares responsibility for a movement that was dependent for its very existence on the cooperation of men and women from all sections of society.

Since crusading was far more embedded in Christian history than nearly everyone in the West now wants to believe, one purpose of this book is to draw attention to the gulf that has opened up between the historical actuality perceived by specialists in the subject and modern convictions. I will try to explain how the Crusades were viewed in religious terms by the Christian faithful, how the language associated with them was appropriated by Europeans in the age of imperialism, and how the nineteenth-century rhetoric, itself a distortion of reality, was in the twentieth century distorted again both in the West and in Islam.

—————

The author of a tract entitled *The Reality of the New Crusaders War*, which was written to justify the atrocity of September 11, 2001, gave himself the *nom de plume* of "Saladin, Defeater of the Crusaders."[17] The spectacular events of recent years have inspired several crusade historians to provide some explanation of the Salafist *jihadis'* perception of crusading and of their employment of the word "crusade" in their propaganda. In my case the starting point was an invitation in 2002 by The Old Dominion University, Norfolk, Virginia, to give a lecture on the first anniversary of the massacre of so many innocent civilians in New York.[18] I used some of the arguments in this book relating to the nineteenth and twentieth centuries then, and later developed them elsewhere, but here they are combined with others and are deployed in a more comprehensive attempt to place the Crusades in Christian history and to understand the long-term effects in the West and among Muslims of the use, and misuse, of crusade ideas and images. It will be noticed that I owe a great deal to Elizabeth Siberry, who in pioneering works, similar to those of Kenneth Setton on the sixteenth and seventeenth centuries,[19] has drawn attention to much of the nineteenth-century material[20] and to Werner Ende, Carole Hillenbrand, and Emmanuel Sivan, who have revealed the rich sources in modern Arabic historiography.[21] But my message is my own. It is that we cannot hope to comprehend—and thereby confront—those who hate us so much unless we understand how they are thinking; and this involves opening our eyes to the actuality—not the imagined reality—of our own past.

This book is, with some slight alterations and reorganization, the Bampton Lectures in America, which I was honored to give at Columbia University in October 2007. I cannot end without thanking Professor Robert Somerville, the Department of Religion at Columbia, and the Trustees of the Bampton Lectures in America for giving me the opportunity to deliver them.

CHAPTER ONE

Crusades as Christian Holy Wars

Crusades were penitential war pilgrimages, fought not only in the Levant and throughout the eastern Mediterranean region, but also along the Baltic shoreline, in North Africa, the Iberian Peninsula, Poland, Hungary and the Balkans, and even within Western Europe. They were proclaimed not only against Muslims, but also against pagan Wends, Balts and Lithuanians, shamanist Mongols, Orthodox Russians and Greeks, Cathar and Hussite heretics, and those Catholics whom the church deemed to be its enemies. The crusading movement generated holy leagues, which were alliances of front-line powers, bolstered by crusade privileges, and military orders, the members of which sometimes operated out of their own order-states.

It is the length of time crusading lasted and its expression in many different theaters of war that make it so hard to define.[1] It was adaptable and aspects of it changed in response to circumstances and even fashion, but certain elements were constant. To crusade meant to engage in a war that was both holy, because it was believed to be waged on God's behalf, and penitential, because those taking part considered themselves to be performing an act of penance. The war was authorized by the pope as vicar of Christ. Most crusaders were lay men and women who made vows, committing themselves to join an expedition. When their vows were fulfilled, or when a campaign was considered to have ended, the individuals concerned resumed their normal lives. There were also crusaders of another type, the brothers (and in some cases sisters) of the military orders—such as the Knights Templar, Knights Hospitaller, and Teutonic Knights—who made vows of profession and were therefore permanently engaged in the defense of Christians and Christendom. The vows, whether specific and temporary, varying a little from place to place and over time, or permanent ones of profession into a military order, were symbolized by the wearing of crosses, either on everyday clothes or on religious habits. The lay men and women who made them were rewarded with indulgences, guarantees that the penitential act in which they were engaged would rank in God's eyes as a fully satisfactory remission of the sins that they had committed up to that date.[2] It is against these basic features that every manifestation, or pseudomanifestation, of the movement must be measured.

The body of inspired writings that Christians consider to be divine revelation is ambivalent when it comes to the use of violence, by which I mean physical actions that threaten, whether intentionally or as side effects, homicide or injury to the human body. On Mount Sinai, Moses received from God the commandment "You shall not kill," but what struck fourth-century Christian theologians was how, in the narrative of events on and around Sinai, that commandment was immediately modified. In the book of the Covenant that follows and is a gloss upon the Ten Commandments, God was reported demanding the death penalty for an inventory of crimes and promising to exterminate those peoples who barred the entry of the Israelites into the Promised Land. When Moses came down from Sinai with the Tablets of the Law and found his followers worshipping a golden calf, he was described authorizing their slaughter.[3]

It is a mistake to assume that the New Testament unequivocally condemns the use of force. Christ did indeed demand of his followers love of enemies as well as friends, meekness, gentleness, and nonresistance. On the other hand, he, like John the Baptist, seemed to accept the need for soldiers, as when he praised the faith of the centurion but did not question his profession.[4] And at the end of the Last Supper, according to St. Luke, he told the apostles: "'Let him who has no sword sell his mantle and buy one. For I tell you that this scripture must be fulfilled in me, *And he was reckoned with transgressors* . . .' And they said, 'Look, Lord, here are two swords.' And he said to them, 'It is enough.'"[5] Later in the evening his followers were carrying swords, presumably those from the room, and it must have been with one of these that St. Peter cut off the ear of the high priest's servant.[6] Peter was rebuked by Christ, but, the war theorists asked, if Christ had been opposed to the use of force on principle, what was his leading disciple doing walking at his side bearing a sword, even if the purpose was to fulfill scripture?[7] Other New Testament texts, particularly those relating to the career of St. Paul, recognized the use of force by the state. The ruler in authority "does not bear the sword in vain [wrote Paul]; he is the servant of God to execute his wrath on the wrongdoer."[8]

It was in an attempt to resolve the contradictions in scripture that the moral theology of violence evolved. Pacifism had played some, perhaps a significant, part in the early church, although its extent has now been questioned.[9] It survived as a minority opinion throughout the centuries that followed—we shall see that crusade preachers felt the need to answer its root-and-branch objections—but once their coreligionists became more numerous and occupied ranks in the army, posts in the judiciary involving the imposition of penal sanctions, and the imperial throne itself, Christian thinkers had to face up to the issues involved. They found no comfort in distinguishing the old dispensation from the new, not only because the new dispensation was itself ambivalent, but also because if the state of mankind and of man's perception of God had led him to authorize violence in one era, the fact that he frowned on much of it in another could not in any way prevent him from changing his policy again if conditions here on earth merited it.

For more than 2,000 years of Western history, violence, whether expressed in warfare, armed rebellion, or the employment of force as a state sanction, and whether holy or merely licit, has required three criteria to be considered legitimate. First, it must not be entered into lightly or for aggrandizement, but only for a legally sound reason, which has to be a reactive one. Second, it must be formally declared by an authority recognized as having the power to make such a declaration. Third, it must be waged justly. These principles, rooted in the law of the Roman Republic, were developed in a Christian context by St. Augustine of Hippo, the greatest of the early theoreticians, who wrote at the turn of the fourth and fifth centuries.[10] Augustine defined the offense that provided violence with a *just cause* as intolerable injury, usually taking the form of aggression or oppression. Since injuries disturbed earthly order, which reflected the divine order, resistance to them was a stern necessity for good men. "It is [Augustine wrote] the injustice of the opposing side that lays on the wise man the duty to wage wars."[11]

He recognized two expressions of *legitimate authority*. He followed St. Paul in treating all rulers, even pagan ones, as divine ministers, although he saw the Christian Roman emperors especially as representatives of God, who had put them and the temporal power of the empire at the Church's disposal for its defense. But he also believed that God could personally order violence, which would be "without doubt just."[12] On divine authority Abraham had been prepared to sacrifice Isaac, and Moses had waged war. God, in mandating the use of force, acted not out of cruelty but in righteous retribution.[13] Augustine's fullest treatment of the subject of divinely ordained violence is to be found in his *Contra Faustum Manichaeum*, a defense of the Old Testament in reply to the Manichees, but he was prepared for direct commands from God to be transmitted to men under the new dispensation, and he referred to the possibility of them coming in his own time in two of his later works.[14]

He was at his most positive when writing about the *right intention* required of those who authorized and took part in violence. They had to be motivated by love and should only use as much force as necessary. It followed that those responsible for the management of violence should circumscribe it in such a way that the innocent suffered as little as possible.[15] Augustine's treatment of right intention provided the foundations for the later doctrine of proportionality.

I have given his ideas more clarity than would have been apparent to his contemporaries or even perhaps to himself, since they were scattered throughout a vast corpus, written over several decades, and were sometimes contradictory. It was not until the eleventh century, when the popes turned to learned supporters to justify the use of force on the church's behalf, that citations from Augustine's works were anthologized in a convenient form with the contradictions ironed out.[16] This process brought into focus two premises that underpinned his treatment of violence. The first was an insistence on the ultimate authority of a God or Christ who was intimately involved in the affairs of this dimension. It was in his name and in accordance with his wishes that his ministers authorized the use of force, in order to prevent his will being frustrated. The second was the conviction that violence was ethically neutral. What was evil in war of itself? Augustine had asked. The real evils were not the deaths of those who would have died anyway, but the love of violence, cruelty, and enmity; it was generally to punish such that good men undertook wars in obedience to God or to some lawful authority.[17] It was the intention of the perpetrators, therefore, that provided force with a moral dimension—bad in many cases, but good in some—and this led Augustine to develop a theory of just persecution that was to haunt Christian history up until the nineteenth century.[18]

The Augustinian tradition seems so alien today because it has been displaced by another set of ideas, which reached maturity much more recently than we like to think. Modern just war theory presumes, unlike Augustine, that violence is indeed an evil, but also that disorder can be a greater one. The use of force may therefore become a necessity as the lesser of evils when a state or community is faced with a situation in which order can only be restored by means of it. In these special circumstances it will be condoned by God and participation in it will not incur guilt. The origins of this body of thought are to be found in the Middle Ages, when theologians and canon lawyers struggled with demands for advice coming from those engaged in conflicts that were not covered by any traditional model,[19] but the theory could not make headway until a consensus was prepared to abandon the Augustinian premises. Catalysts for the jettisoning of the belief that force could be employed on Christ's behalf were reports in the 1530s of atrocities committed by the Spaniards against the indigenous peoples in the New World and the critical reaction to them of Francisco de Vitoria, who rejected the notion that violence could be part of any divine plan. He and his followers could only justify it by reference to the Aristotelian and Thomist idea of "the common good," the defense of which was the prerogative of every community. Christ began to withdraw from the fray as just war arguments moved from the field of moral theology to that of international law.[20]

If you had asked most Enlightenment thinkers, for many of whom the Crusades were "ces guerres horribles,"[21] how they could justify war, they would probably have replied that in some cases the requirements of a foreseeable good—the common good—could outweigh predictably evil results. The evil they referred to, however, was not the violence itself but the suffering that accompanied it. Although there was general agreement that the use of force nearly always had unpleasant consequences and great interest was expressed in the measures that might be taken to ameliorate them, there seems to have been no serious intellectual challenge to the consensus that violence was morally neutral.[22] No one seems to have taken the second step necessary for the full emergence of modern just war theory, the borrowing from pacifism of the conviction that violence is intrinsically evil. The topic still needs research, but I suspect that this very important shift in thought was an achievement of a popular and widespread peace movement that swept Europe and America after the Napoleonic Wars.

Holy war, of which there are many examples in Christian history, may be defined as being considered to be authorized directly or indirectly by God (or Christ) and as being fought to further what are believed to be his intentions.[23] Crusades were particularly theatrical manifestations of it, but, although the reasons for them could not in the eyes of contemporaries have been more weighty, since they involved the removal of impediments to God's wishes for humankind, they were still expected to be subject to the same criteria of just cause, legitimate authority, and right intention as should be all expressions of Christian violence. In a sermon preached to the brothers of a military order early in the thirteenth century, the preacher James of Vitry summarized the first of these criteria as the repelling of violence or injury and the imposition of justice on wrongdoers.[24] In other words, the Crusades, like all Christian wars, had to be reactive; they could never, for example, be wars of conversion, although popes and preachers sometimes sailed close to the wind in their anxiety to gain recruits for campaigns in support of missions in the Baltic region, where the traditions were muscular, and crusaders elsewhere could be very ignorant of canon law.[25] Even crusading wars against heretics were justified as reactive ones, since the heretics had chosen to rebel against Christ's establishment of the church as the custodian of truths that they had once recognized.[26]

The cause for a crusade was a particularly important matter, because a war of this kind was fought primarily not by those performing feudal service or by conscripts (although there were often conscripts in the armies), but by volunteers. Crusaders were such by virtue of the vows they had made, as we have seen, and in canon law a vow had to be a voluntary act.[27] When, therefore, a pope proclaimed a crusade, this could be no more than an appeal to men and women to join an expedition of their own free will. He might threaten them with hell-fire, but he could not force them to make vows, or punish them if they did not, and there were occasions when efforts at recruitment failed. A convincing case was therefore essential. When in the early 1270s the Dominican preacher Humbert of Romans set out to answer what appeared to him to be seven kinds of objection put forward by critics of the Crusades to the East, four related to the cause and illustrate that the concerns of his audiences were not too different from those we would come across today. Some people were arguing that "it is not in accordance with the Christian religion to shed blood in this way, even that of wicked infidels." Others were anxious about preemption, since "although we have a duty to defend ourselves against the Muslims when they attack us, it does not seem that we ought to attack their lands or their persons when they leave us in peace; and it does not seem that this can be done without committing an injury." Concern was also being expressed at the disparity between the numbers of Christians and Muslims involved, at the alien nature of the ground on which the crusaders would have to fight, and about the climate and the food available to them, so that "it looks as though we are putting God to the test." There were doubts whether there was any point in sending expeditions to the Levant, particularly as it was difficult to get Europeans to colonize any lands that were conquered.[28] To Humbert's list could be added the storms of protest whipped up by the supporters of crusading in other theaters of war, convinced that their causes were the most pressing, that greeted any decision by the papacy to concentrate resources on a particular front.[29]

So the case for each expedition had to be a good one and a feature of papal general letters was the care taken in arguing it as cogently as possible. Expeditions to the Levant, North Africa, or the Iberian Peninsula could be justified as responses to present Muslim aggression or as rightful attempts to recover Christian territory which had been injuriously seized in the past. The need to recover and hold Jerusalem, containing the two most sacred locations in Christendom, the Holy Sepulchre and Calvary, was a powerful incentive. As the preacher John of Abbeville put it in c. 1217, quoting from Scripture the words *Our inheritance has turned over to strangers, our homes to aliens,* "the Land of Promise is our *inheritance* and the place where Christ was buried and suffered is our *home.* And this inheritance is given into the hands of the gentiles. . . . Now our holy inheritance is seized; the holy places are profaned; the holy cross is made a captive."[30]

The goal of Jerusalem was also used to reinforce the case for crusades in the Iberian Peninsula, because many Spaniards had convinced themselves that the best route to the Holy Land was by way of Spain and North Africa.[31] Campaigns along the Baltic were portrayed, sometimes rather spuriously, as reactions to the threat to Christian settlements posed by the pagan Balts and Lithuanians.[32] Wars against heretics and political opponents of the papacy were launched to counter an internal and active menace to the unity of Christendom or the security of the church.[33] Peter the Venerable, the influential abbot of Cluny, argued that violence against fellow Christians was even more justifiable than the use of force against infidels: "Whom is it better for you and yours to fight, the pagan who does not know God or the Christian who, confessing him in words, battles against him in deeds?

Whom is it better to proceed against, the man who is ignorant and blasphemous or the man who knows the truth and is aggressive?"[34]

The authority legitimizing crusades, which were often euphemistically called his "business" (*negotium Christi*), was believed to be Christ himself. It was this, of course, that made them holy wars. As the vicar of Christ and also, as Pope Innocent IV put it, the heir of the Roman emperors,[35] the pope was responsible for their public proclamation. Although the necessity for papal authorization was not widely recognized until the 1140s and the concept of the vicariate of Christ did not become prominent until about the same time,[36] the first crusaders were already certain that Pope Urban II had summoned them to war on Christ's behalf. Before his departure for the East in 1096, Count Robert II of Flanders claimed to be "responding to a divine command published by the authority of the apostolic see."[37] Writing to Urban from Syria in 1098, the crusade leaders referred to the pope as "you who originated this journey and by your speeches made us all leave our lands and whatever was in them and ordered us to follow Christ carrying our crosses"; they asked him to "fulfil what you have encouraged us to do" and complete "the journey of Jesus Christ begun by us and preached by you" and "the war which is your own."[38]

The success of the First Crusade reinforced the belief that the pope's proclamation had been divinely inspired. Those who took part and those who remained at home became convinced that the only explanation for the victorious progress of an army so short of provisions and material, and so weighed down by noncombatants, was that God had intervened.[39] Commentators dwelt on the crusade's miraculous nature and the unique way its course had demonstrated divine approval: "Apart from the mystery of the healing cross, what more marvellous deed has there been since the creation of the world than that which was achieved in modern times in this journey of *Jerosolimitani*?"[40] The reports of Urban's proclamation of war at Clermont in November 1095, written after the triumphant seizure of Jerusalem nearly four years later, were full of references to Christ's personal authority.

It ought to be a beautiful ideal for you to die for Christ in that city where Christ died for you, but if it should happen that you should die here, you may be sure that it will be as if you had died on the way, provided, that is, Christ finds you in his company of knights. . . . You ought to fight for such an emperor, who is all powerful and who lacks none of the rewards with which to repay you.[41]

The portrayal of an endangered Christ personally calling on men to hurry to his aid became a powerful theme in crusade preaching. In a sermon delivered in Basel on May 3, 1200, Abbot Martin of Pairis entrusted Christ's person to the crusaders: "And so, strong warriors, run to Christ's aid today, enlist in the knighthood of Christ, hasten to band yourselves together in companies sure of success. It is to you today that I commit Christ's cause, it is into your hands that I give over, so to speak, Christ himself, so that you may strive to restore him to his inheritance, from which he has been cruelly expelled."[42] A few years later Pope Innocent III drew attention in a characteristically blunt manner to the consequences of failing to help Christ when he needed assistance:

Because at this time there is a more compelling urgency than there has ever been before to help the Holy Land in her great need and because we hope that the aid sent to her will be greater than that which has ever reached her before, listen when, again taking up the old cry, we cry to you. We cry on behalf of him who when dying cried *with a loud voice* on the cross, becoming *obedient* to God the father *unto death on a cross*, crying out so that he might snatch us from the crucifixion of eternal death. . . . He has granted [men] an opportunity to win salvation, nay more, a means of salvation, so that those who fight faithfully for him will be crowned in happiness by him, but those who refuse to pay him the servant's service they owe him in a crisis of such great urgency will justly deserve to suffer a sentence of damnation on the Last Day of Severe Judgement.[43]

At the time of the First Crusade, Christ could be portrayed as a father summoning his children to his aid in a vendetta to recover property that had been wrongfully taken from him: "I address fathers and sons and brothers and nephews. If an outsider were to strike one of you down would you not avenge your blood-relation? How much more ought you to avenge your God, your father, your brother, whom you see reproached, banished from his estates, crucified!"[44] As the twelfth century progressed this image was overtaken by that of Christ as a king or feudal lord calling for service from his subjects or vassals. This featured in papal general letters[45] and was echoed by preachers like James of Vitry:

> The Lord really has been afflicted by the loss of his patrimony. He wishes to test his friends and to see whether his vassals are faithful. If anyone holds a fief of a liege-lord and deserts him when he is attacked and loses his inheritance, that vassal should rightly be deprived of his fief. You hold your body, your soul, and everything you have from the highest emperor. Today he has had you summoned to hurry to his aid in battle.[46]

Crusaders were, therefore, soldiers called upon to take to the field on Christ's behalf, although we shall see later that they were expected to achieve more for themselves than armed service. James of Vitry assured his listeners that the bearing of arms was something God often required:

> On this matter Augustine wrote, "Do not think that anyone who serves in warlike arms cannot please God; among these was holy David, among these was that centurion who said in the gospel of Luke, *Lord I am not worthy to have you come under my roof. I have soldiers under me* (Matt. 8:8−9 or Luke 7:6−8). The Lord pointed to him as a witness, because he had not found such great faith in Israel. So when you are armed for battle, first remember this, that your strength, your physical strength itself, is a gift from God."[47]

The notion of military service was familiar to European knights, of course, and it tended to be theatrically and ostentatiously expressed. John of Ibelin, count of Jaffa, arrived in Egypt to join the crusade of King Louis IX of France

> most nobly of all, for his galley came painted below the waterline and above with escutcheons of his arms. . . . He had at least 300 oarsmen in his galley and by each bench there was a shield upon which were his arms; and to each shield there was attached a pennon on which were his arms beaten in gold. And as he approached it seemed as though his galley flew as the oarsmen drove it forward and it seemed as if lightning were falling from the skies at the sound made by the pennons and by cymbals, drums and Saracen horns.[48]

Display was a feature of chivalric society against which churchmen fought hard. The popes made clear their disapproval of luxury and extravagance, and they could not resist addressing enthusiasts in deflating terms, such as those Innocent III directed at Duke Leopold VI of Austria:

> There is much more merit in the gibbet of Christ's cross than in the little sign of yours. . . . For you accept a soft and gentle cross; he suffered one that was bitter and hard. You bear it superficially on your clothing; he endured his in the reality of his flesh. You sew yours on with linen or silk threads; he was fastened to his with hard, iron nails.[49]

There was obviously a connection between crusading and chivalric culture, which appeared on the scene at about the same time and grew to maturity alongside the Crusades. The knights who were most admired in chivalric society were often enthusiastic crusaders. Philip Daubeny, buried in 1236 by the south door of the church of the Holy Sepulchre, which had only recently been restored to Latin Christian control, was considered in England to be a paragon of chivalry.[50] He had been appointed "*magister et eruditor*" to the young King Henry III. He had been administrator, diplomat, and field commander in England, Gascony, and the Channel Islands. He was rich, loyal, honest, able, and above all, he was committed to the cause of the Holy Land. The son of a man who had died on the Third Crusade, he himself took the cross three times. According to the chronicler Matthew Paris, who did not generally hold crusaders in esteem, "he deserved burial in the Holy Land, which he had long desired during his life."[51] But chivalry, an essentially nonreligious movement that, perhaps subconsciously, parodied religion, coexisted rather uneasily with crusading.[52] The pomp, the banners, and the coats-of-arms displayed on campaign were trappings, which may have helped to make the reality—the dust, mud, violence, starvation, disease, and death—easier to bear, but could never displace the elements at the heart of the crusade ethos that truly defined it. These included a particular interpretation of right intention, the third of the principles constraining Christian violence.

We have seen that for Augustine of Hippo right intention manifested itself in love. Crusaders were supposed, therefore, to be motivated by Christian charity, although the preachers who recruited them tended to stress love of God and of brothers and sisters in the faith, and for understandable reasons avoided the issue of love of enemies.[53] Love was meant to feature especially in the lives and actions of the brothers of the military orders, the first of which, the Knights Templar, had been founded in 1120. Pope Innocent II wrote to them a few years later: "Like true Israelites and warriors most versed in holy battle, on fire with the flame of true love, you carry out in your deeds the words of the Gospel, in which it is said *Greater love has no man than this, that a man lay down his life for his friends* (John 15:13)."[54]

The relationship between love and violence has never been an easy one, whatever Augustine of Hippo believed, and it is clear that the transformation of the Hospital of St. John of Jerusalem into a military order was a traumatic process.[55] The order had originated as an entirely pacific institution: the brothers had been inspired to serve the poor and had made their ideal a reality by ministering to pilgrims when they were sick and burying them when they died. It took the first steps toward militarization as early as the 1120s, but differences within the community in Jerusalem surfaced in 1169, when it was nearly bankrupted by expensive long-term military commitments and the master resigned.[56] Most of the brothers, appalled at what they considered to be needless expenditure, insisted, with the support of Pope Alexander III, that frontier castles should not be acquired and important agreements should not be entered into without the consent of chapter, but, there was more to their concern than finance.[57] Factions within the central convent had still not been reconciled a decade later, when their opinions were reflected in two papal letters that, as was so often the case, were echoing opinions that had been transmitted to the apostolic see by the parties concerned. In the first, Alexander stated that the Hospitallers' prime obligation was to care for the poor and that they should not be diverted into military enterprises except on very special occasions. The hospital, he added, had been instituted for the reception and refection of the poor and it should concentrate on those duties, "especially as it is believed that the poor are better defended by showing them love and mercy than by force of arms."[58] At almost the same time, however, his curia reissued one of the order's most important early privileges, in which passages borrowed from an earlier charter for the Templars and describing a military function were interpolated. This hybrid letter formally legitimated the order's military role for the first time.[59]

The Hospitaller leadership responded to the crisis by stressing that the warfare in which their order was engaged had a symbiotic relationship to the care of the sick poor. A statute of 1181 decreed that their battle standard, which was already doubling as the funeral pall of deceased brothers, was also to cover the biers of poor pilgrims who had died in their hospital.[60] Another statute of 1182, which contained the first overt reference in Hospitaller legislation to a military wing and must have been very carefully worded, blandly associated fighting with acts of mercy: "These are the special charities established in the Hospital, apart from the brothers-at-arms, which the House ought to support honourably, and many other charities which cannot be individually detailed."[61]

The same concern to associate military activities with nursing ones may have given rise to a practice that a German visitor to Jerusalem in the 1180s described. The brother knights, in order to demonstrate that what they had belonged to the sick, had to surrender their warhorses if, in the opinion of the surgeons in the order's mobile field hospital, there were not enough animals available to move the injured in the aftermath of battle.[62]

The dispute in the Hospitaller central convent had not been about the morality of warfare, but it had shown that it was not easy to persuade members of a religious institute to engage at the same time in two disparate activities, although it is significant that the solution found was not to abandon one of them, but to link them more closely together.

≈≈≈

For churchmen—and indeed for most laymen, however they might behave—to crusade was to engage in a serious business, dangerous, debilitating, and impoverishing, and one that was, as I will describe in the next chapter, primarily a penitential exercise. It was also to enter for a divine examination. The idea of the summons to take the cross as God's own test of an individual put it on a different plane from those feats of knightly endurance in fiction that appealed so much to contemporaries. However, when it was first proposed by Bernard of Clairvaux in the 1140s it was presented as providing an occasion for celebration.

> [God] puts himself into a position of necessity, or pretends to be in one, so that he can award those fighting for him wages: the remission of their sins and everlasting glory. It is because of this that I have called you a blessed generation, you who have been caught up in a time so rich in remission and are found living in this year so pleasing to the Lord, truly a year of jubilee.[63]

After the disasters that struck in 1187, when Jerusalem and much of the Holy Land was lost to the Muslims, the tone of churchmen became much more minatory.

> The Lord, indeed, could save [the Holy Land] by his will alone, but it is not for us to ask why he has acted thus. For perhaps the Lord has wished to find out and bring to the notice of others whether there is anyone who has knowledge of him or is seeking

after him and might joyfully embrace the chance of penitence offered to him and in laying down his life for his brothers may be killed in a brief moment and gain eternal life.[64]

The portrayal of the crusade as a test was closely associated with the conviction, inspired by Old Testament examples, that success or failure was to be attributed less to the crusaders than to the divine will. Writing to King Alfonso VIII of Castile after the great victory over the Almohads at Las Navas de Tolosa in 1212, Innocent III reminded him that he should humbly confess

> that it was not your highness's hands but the Lord who has done all these things. . . . For that victory took place without doubt not by human but by divine agency; and the sword of God, not of man . . . destroyed the enemies of the cross. . . . So do not walk proudly because those who work wickedness have fallen there, but give glory and honour to the Lord, saying humbly with the prophet *the zeal of the Lord of Hosts* has done *this.*[65]

Three and a half centuries later a humble surrender to God's will was supposed to account for the unity that prevailed in the Christian fleet before the victory at Lepanto in 1571: "Without for a moment giving heed or thought to death they prepared to fight for Jesus Christ, to such an extent that suddenly one saw a mighty mystery and a miraculous demonstration of God's supreme power."[66]

It followed that when little was achieved or when disaster struck, the instruments at God's disposal had proved themselves to be unworthy of him. "The Lord seems to have been provoked by our sins. . . . He has not spared his people, not even his own name."[67] Crusaders all too often found themselves both heroes and villains: lauded when they took the cross, but subject to excoriation if they were considered to have failed.[68] And since failure was a judgment on the whole of Christian society, concern was regularly expressed about the spiritual health not only of those on crusade, but also of the faithful in general. The belief that any chance of extraliminal victory could be vitiated by corruption or divisions at home, so that only when society was unde-

filed and was practicing uniformly true religion could a war on its behalf be successful, was being widely expressed following the catastro-
phe of 1187. "It is incumbent upon all of us [wrote Pope Gregory
VIII] to consider and to choose to amend our sins by voluntary chas-
tizement and to turn to the Lord our God with penance and works of
piety; and we should first amend in ourselves what we have done
wrong and then turn our attention to the treachery and malice of the
enemy."[69]

It was no coincidence, therefore, that the loss of Jerusalem in 1187
was a prelude to a series of crusades launched inward against deviants
within Christendom.[70] The fact is that holy war, whatever the religion involved, has the tendency to turn in on the society that has bred
it. In the twelfth-century Near East there was a movement for moral
rearmament, associated with a *jihad* that was being waged against the
crusaders, as we will see later. This came to prominence under Nur
ad-Din, the ruler of Damascus and Egypt, and was marked by the
building of *madrasas* and the suppression of heresies, particularly
Shi'ism.[71] In nineteenth-century Java, Dipanagra, the leader of a religious revolt against all foreigners and unbelievers that, after a short
purifying period of violence, ought to have culminated in his rule as
the millenarian "just king," wanted to impose strict confessional uniformity.[72] The twentieth-century Vietnamese Hoa Hao sect, which
had inherited radical millenarian warlike Buddhism and flourished
among the peasants in the Mekong Delta, pursued the same goal, as
do the twenty-first-century Salafist *jihadis*.[73] A historian who has stud-
ied various millenarian anticolonial movements—in Java, New Zea-
land, India, German East Africa, and Burma—has concluded that in
all of them there was the desire to purge alien groups from within
their own societies.[74]

Crusading was not generally millenarian, but it was typical of holy
warfare in that introspection increased in relation to failure abroad.
One reaction was to accuse men perceived to be the opponents of the
church of undermining the movement, as when Innocent III proclaimed a crusade in 1199 against Markward of Anweiler, the Staufen
representative in Sicily: "We concede to all who fight the violence of
Markward and his army the same remission of sins which we grant to

all who arm themselves to fight the perfidy of the Muslims in defence of the eastern province, since aid to the Holy Land is hindered through his actions."[75]

Associated with this was the need felt to eliminate nonconformity, which manifested itself in a drive to impose uniformity on Western society, which was already remarkably monocultural. When calling for a crusade against the heretical Cathars in 1208, in language replete with the imagery of uncleanliness and disease, Innocent summoned the "knights of Christ . . . to wipe out the treachery of heresy and its followers by attacking the heretics with a strong hand and an outstretched arm, that much more confidently than you would attack the Muslims because [the heretics] are worse than them."[76] This was obviously not the first occasion on which force had been used against the popes' political enemies or authorized against heretics, but within forty years men who had taken the cross for the East were finding themselves being pressured to commute their vows in favor of internal police actions, and this redirection against enemies within Christendom of armies originally engaged to confront external threats was a novelty.[77]

It may well be that the earliest example of introspective violence associated with crusading was the persecution of Jewish communities in Western Europe by departing crusaders in 1096. Although there were outbreaks of violent anti-Judaism in France and in Eastern Europe, the worst atrocities occurred in the Rhineland, where the Jewish community at Mainz, one of the largest in Europe, was decimated.[78] Thereafter, for more than a century, the preaching of every major crusade to the East generated anti-Jewish pogroms somewhere in the West, and it is not surprising that Jewish leaders became very nervous when crusades were in preparation. The irony was that the Jews were members of the only officially protected non-Christian community in Western society. The bewildering language of leading churchmen,[79] who expressed their abhorrence of them, often in emotive terms, while at the same time ring-fencing them in a way denied to heretics, so confused the faithful that the bishops often found themselves in the situation of shepherds trailing after flocks that had run amok, because the pressure to extend introspective violence to all non-Catholic communities was coming from below. I am now inclined to think that, in the context of the calls to cleanse and purify the Christian sanctuaries in Palestine that permeate the sources, the baptisms that were being forced on the Jews in 1096 had the aim of creating a uniformly Christian society by eliminating their religion. The writer Ekkehard of Aura reported that the intention of the persecutors was to wipe out the Jewish communities or compel them to enter the church, and there are other references to the abomination of allowing these aliens to coexist with Christians within Western Europe.[80]

Nearly everything about the Crusades I have described so far, including the tendency to turn on those perceived to be deviants at home, could have been present at least theoretically in other forms of Christian holy warfare, although nowhere else were the ideas relating to warfare itself expressed as coherently or attractively to so many contemporaries. But there were exceptions to the norms of holy warfare, and two of them—the establishment of the military orders and the insistence that the crusaders take vows—were expressions of a characteristic of crusading that made it very nearly unique, the fact that it involved the waging of penitential warfare. This feature was so important in defining the movement and inspiring recruits that it deserves a chapter to itself.

CHAPTER TWO

Crusades as Christian Penitential Wars

In his account of the First Crusade the monk-historian Guibert of Nogent, who had not taken part himself, recalled the behavior of a knight named Matthew, whose family were vassals of Guibert's parents. Guibert had heard of the scrupulous care with which Matthew, whom he believed had died a martyr, had followed the religious observances of a pilgrimage.[1] Matthew was exceptional, of course, but all crusaders were expected to behave as though they were penitents on pilgrimage. A list of regulations, drawn up by Rhinelander, Flemish, and English crusaders sailing from Dartmouth on May 23, 1147, included decrees against extravagant dress and on the confinement of women to the living quarters; on the keeping of peace; on weekly chapters, to be held separately by the clergy and the laity and on general meetings should the need for them arise; and on weekly confession and communion. Each ship in the fleet was to be treated as a parish and was to have its own "parish priest."[2]

For at least the first three centuries of the movement, care was taken to give all theaters of war pilgrimage credentials. I have already pointed out that there was a conviction in the Iberian Peninsula that the best route to Jerusalem was through Spain and North Africa.

Some crusades against the political enemies of the church in Italy were described as pilgrimages on the grounds that Rome, itself a major pilgrim center, was threatened or that the way to the Holy Land had to be cleared before it could be recovered.[3] Heretics were portrayed as not only menacing the church and angering God, but also, as we have seen, impeding crusades to the Holy Land by diverting the energies and concentration of the faithful elsewhere.[4] In the Baltic region the fiction was maintained in the thirteenth century that the territory around Riga was the patrimony of the Blessed Virgin Mary, to be treated with the same reverence as was the patrimony of Christ in Palestine.[5]

When not in armor crusaders were supposed to dress simply as pilgrims. A sculpture that once stood in the cloister of the priory of Belval in Lorraine portrays Count Hugh I of Vaudémont, who accompanied King Louis VII of France to the East in 1147, wearing simple traveling garments, although his staff and purse—the symbols of pilgrimage—and the cross sewn on the front of his cloak show him to have been a crusader.[6] In 1099, after the liberation of Jerusalem, the survivors of the First Crusade apparently threw most of their weapons and armor away and returned to Europe carrying only the palm fronds they had collected, as evidence that they had completed their pilgrimage.[7] One of them, Count Rotrou of Mortagne, deposited his palms, which clearly had great emotional significance, on the altar in his family's foundation, the abbey of Nogent-le-Rotrou.[8]

As late as the twelfth century a spectrum of opinion ranged from doubts, expressed by what was now a small minority, as to whether sin could be avoided in acts of war to the conviction that participation in altruistic violence could be virtuous and that resulting death could even lead to martyrdom.[9] The vision of warrior-martyrs in a holy war predated crusading, and was therefore not a defining characteristic, but from 1096 onward it featured prominently in crusade propaganda and popular belief.[10] John of Joinville felt passionately that King Louis IX of France, whom he had accompanied to the East in 1248, should have been canonized not as a confessor but as a martyr, because of his death before Tunis in 1270.[11] Louis himself and Charles of Anjou believed that their brother Robert of Artois had died a martyr's death in the battle of Mansurah in 1250.[12] It was, of course, one thing for the public to hold to the dubious proposition that warriors, whose internal dispositions in the heat of battle could not be gauged, should be ranked with those who died passively for the faith, and quite another for the church to include them in its calendars of saints. It never did so, but the need even senior churchmen felt to temporize when confronted by the convictions of the laity is illustrated by two sermons commemorating the deaths of Robert of Artois and his companions, probably preached in Acre by Eudes of Châteauroux, the papal legate, on the first anniversary of the battle. In one, which appears to have been delivered to an audience of French lay nobles who had fought at Mansurah, including perhaps King Louis himself, Eudes did refer to the dead as martyrs, although he pointed out that "there are different kinds of martyrdom" and allowed himself a way out of his predicament by asking God's forgiveness for those "who, prevented by fear of suffering, did not perhaps accept death in the state of devotion in which they ought to have been." In the other sermon, probably delivered before the clergy, there is no reference to martyrdom at all.[13]

The church faced no such problems with the concept of penitential warfare. It was not called upon to declare that a fighter who died on crusade was in heaven, because no one but God and perhaps the individual concerned could be sure that all the conditions for a satisfactory penance had been fulfilled.[14] The idea of fighting "for the remission of sins" was probably unprecedented in the early 1080s, when it had come to feature in the language of Pope Gregory VII and his supporters, who apparently believed that personal engagement in just warfare was so meritorious that the danger involved could be treated as a penance.[15] It would never have been easy to justify the inflicting of pain and loss of life on others, with the consequential distortion of the perpetrator's internal dispositions, as a penance simply because the penitent was exposing himself to danger—however unpleasant the experience might have been for him—and Gregory's opponents were predictably critical.[16] When Pope Urban II preached the First Crusade ten years later, however, he gave the idea a context in which it could be presented more convincingly, because he associated the forthcoming military campaign with the most charismatic of all traditional penances, the pilgrimage to Jerusalem. As penitential events, pilgrimages were "effectively satisfactory," according to the preacher Gilbert of Tournai, "because just as a man has used all parts of his body when he has sinned, so he gives satisfaction by making all his members work hard."[17] With respect to the First Crusade, therefore, the dangers of war gave added value to the penitential merit gained by a pilgrim.[18]

It would be hard to exaggerate how revolutionary this was.[19] A contemporary exclaimed that: "God has instituted in our time holy wars, so that the order of knights and the crowd running in their wake . . . might find a new way of gaining salvation."[20] If the First Crusade had failed there can be little doubt that senior churchmen would have arisen out of the shadows to condemn it, but with its triumph doubts about penitential warfare evaporated. Contemporaries used in relation to the crusade phrases that until then had been customarily applied only to monks and the monastic profession—the knighthood of Christ, the way of the cross, a journey to the heavenly Jerusalem, spiritual warfare[21]—while in monastic commentaries the association of war and penance was given coherence and intellectual weight.[22] The crusaders, moved by love of God and their neighbor, renouncing wives, children, and earthly possessions, and adopting temporary poverty and chastity, were described as going into a voluntary exile and following the way of the cross—one writer compared the liberation of Jerusalem to Joseph of Arimathea taking Christ down from the cross.[23]

It was for this reason that participation in the First Crusade was considered to be in some sense an alternative to entry into the religious life. Contemporaries portrayed the army on the march as a nomadic abbey, its days and nights punctuated by solemn liturgy, its soldiers dedicated to austerity and brotherhood—"just as in the primitive church, nearly all things were shared in common"[24]—and enduring a religious exile—temporary it is true—that led, as one writer put it, "not [to] a military but a monkish life as far as frugality was concerned."[25] It would be tempting to see this monasticization of war as a rationalization of the apparently miraculous triumph of the crusade in an age in which the monastic life was a measure against which everything tended to be set, were it not for the fact that there is evidence that comparisons between monasticism and crusading were being made even before the armies marched.[26] A century and a half later, the preacher Humbert of Romans maintained that necessary for a crusader were confession, contrition, good counsel, advice from the wise, the disposition of house and goods before departure, the making of a will, the restitution of goods that were not one's own and reconciliation with adversaries, constancy of purpose, the comfort of the saints and the assistance of Christian brothers, abstinence from all sin, a speedy penitence from any sin committed through human frailty while on the march, zeal in punishing any evil in the army, and a preoccupation with the sacred.[27] It is notable how similar many of the conditions on this list were to the obligations required of someone entering a religious community.

It was the belief that crusades were collective acts of penance, repayments through self-punishment of the debts owed to God for sin, which distinguished them from other holy wars. Whereas most Christian holy war demanded the service of God in arms by a devout soldier responding passively to divine command, the crusader was invited to cooperate actively, because everything depended on his decision to undertake the penance of fighting in a campaign in which his obligations, at any rate if completed, would constitute for him an act of condign self-punishment. It is no exaggeration to say that a crusade was for an individual only secondarily about service in arms to God or the benefiting of the church or Christianity; it was primarily about benefiting himself, since he was engaged in an act of self-sanctification.

The power of this conception rested in the long term on the way it answered the concerns of the faithful. The remission of sins was as relevant to survivors as to those facing death, and it was offered to members of a society in which it was almost impossible for a layman of any substance, bound by responsibilities to kindred, clients, and dependants, to avoid serious sin. For hundreds of years Europe remained marked by anxieties about sinfulness and a consequence was the attractiveness to many of crusading, which provided the opportunity to make a fresh start. The continuing appeal of penitential warfare is demonstrated by the way it became institutionalized in the crusade indulgence, which received its definitive formulation around 1200.[28]

According to Humbert of Romans, service to Christ could only be truly effective if it was penitential.[29] Preparations for crusades were always marked by acts of penitence, as when in 1147 King Louis VII of France spent a few hours before his departure among lepers in a leper house.[30] Penitential language reached a peak when Western Christendom was in a state of shock over the loss of Jerusalem in 1187. The tone was set by a papal general letter, which proclaimed a new crusade as an "opportunity for repentance and doing good."[31] Sixty years later a crusader's desire to leave no one behind with a grudge moved King Louis IX of France to establish friar-*enquêteurs* to collect and judge complaints about his own officials,[32] and his companion John of Joinville to summon his seigneurial court to allow the airing of any grievances his vassals might have against him.[33] It was characteristic in its combination of penitential piety and melodrama that when Louis, on crusade for a second time, was dying before Tunis he had himself stretched out on a bed of ashes. In the course of his last night on earth he was heard to sigh in a deep voice, "O Jerusalem. O Jerusalem."[34]

The penitential nature of crusading helps to explain why, after the often revolting violence, the most characteristic feature of any expedition was how liturgical it was. The first crusaders began each new stage of the march barefoot and they fasted before every major engagement. In June 1099 they processed, barefoot and carrying crosses, around the city of Jerusalem, which was still in Muslim hands, visiting the holy places outside the walls.[35] When in 1219 the siege of Damietta in Egypt was going badly, the clergy proclaimed a three-day fast on bread and water and decreed that on every Saturday the army was to process barefoot, singing psalms and the litany.[36] Thirty years further on, John of Joinville's ship left the Roche-de-Marseille for Cyprus with the priests on board singing the *Veni creator spiritus*.[37] Before the battle of Lepanto three hundred years later, "priests, and many galley-captains as well, went from stern to bow with crucifixes in their hands, exhorting and encouraging everybody . . . to consider [Christ] who at that point had descended from heaven to fight against the enemies of his most holy name."[38] Penitential liturgy was not confined to the armies on campaign. Crusaders knew that while they were away a column of prayer would be rising up to heaven from

Western Europe, both intercessory, on their behalf, and penitential, because, as I have already pointed out, failure in God's war would result as much from the faults of men and women on the home front as of those of the fighters. In 1213 a new element was introduced into the rite of the Mass by Pope Innocent III. After the *Pax* all men and women were to prostrate themselves on the ground while Psalm 78 [79]—*O God, the heathen have come into thy inheritance*—was sung or recited, followed by a prayer for the liberation of the Holy Land.[39] A feature of the later Middle Ages was the proliferation of *clamores* and votive Masses on behalf of crusading.[40]

Within a quarter of a century of the First Crusade, professed religious—the brothers of the military orders—were themselves coming to be involved in warfare. Thomas Aquinas was later to justify their existence by pointing out that "fighting in the service of God is imposed on some as a penance, as with those who are enjoined to take up arms in aid of the Holy Land."[41] The military orders were generated by the same movement to reform the religious life as that which gave birth to Cistercians, Carthusians, Premonstratensians, Augustinians, Franciscans, Dominicans, and Carmelites,[42] and the prevailing mood in them was penitential.[43] It is true that the brothers were not averse to employing chivalric theater for a purpose. To encourage European nobles to serve in its wars against the pagan Lithuanians in the fourteenth century, the Teutonic Order stage-managed banquets at Königsberg or Marienburg, at which those knights who had shown the most *prouesse* on campaign were seated at a table of honor and presented with badges by the grand master.[44] But more characteristic was the architecture favored by the Knights Hospitaller on Rhodes. The austerity of their buildings was occasionally broken by moldings over windows or doorways, but the chief decorative feature was provided by coats-of-arms. Splendor was rejected in favor of a severe, almost puritanical, minimalism, identified with nobility and expressing itself in prowess and charity. The message seems to have been that the brothers were embodiments of the ancient Roman virtues of piety and nobility, an idea which had already influenced the learned Hospitaller knight William di Santo Stefano's treatise on law and his order written in the early 1290s.[45] It likewise pervades a little book of advice to a nephew, who had also entered the Order of St. John of Jerusalem, composed in the 1540s by another Hospitaller knight, Sabba di Castiglione.[46]

≈

The appeal of penitential warfare is illustrated amply in the sermons of preachers of the cross. Medieval society, which depended on the internal cohesion provided by kindreds and by the nexuses around lords, did not take kindly to spontaneity. On the other hand, crusade vows, like those on marriage or of profession, were supposed to be voluntary. Few marriages among the arms-bearing classes were entered into spontaneously, of course, but when recruiting crusaders, the preachers knew that they had to persuade their listeners to commit themselves to enterprises that would disrupt their lives, possibly impoverish and even kill or maim them, and inconvenience their families, the support of which they would anyway need if they were to fulfill their promises. So the preachers played on popular concerns and used every technique they could muster to create a sense of theater, an ambience in which commitments would be easier to make.

It was common practice for a preacher to undertake a tour, following the example of the first official recruiter, Pope Urban II, who in his sixties embarked on a year-long journey through France—I estimate that he covered about two thousand miles—entering country towns, the citizens of which had never seen anyone of such international importance in living memory, accompanied by a flock of cardinals, archbishops, and bishops, whose riding households must have been immense and whose train must have stretched across miles of countryside. Crowned with his tiara, the pope rode through the streets before dedicating cathedrals and monastic basilicas with all the liturgical theater that could be employed. And then he preached the cross.[47] Bernard of Clairvaux toured France, Flanders, and the Rhineland fifty years later.[48] In the late 1180s Archbishop Baldwin of Canterbury journeyed around Wales accompanied by interpreters,[49] and Henry of Marcy, the cardinal bishop of Albano, traveled through Germany.[50] In 1213 Pope Innocent III set up an elaborate system of itinerant recruiters in every diocese, who were to assemble "the people of two or three or even more parishes to hear the word of God."[51]

Oliver, the scholastic of Cologne, who was one of them, addressed audiences of thousands.[52] Innocent himself died while on a preaching tour of central Italy in 1216.[53]

The days on which set-piece public sermons were to be delivered were often deliberately chosen. Pope Urban timed his arrival in towns to coincide with great patronal feasts: he was at St. Gilles for the feast of St. Giles, at Le Puy, the greatest Marian shrine of the time, for the feast of the Assumption, and at Poitiers for the feast of St. Hilary.[54] In 1188, for his most important sermon in Germany, Henry of Marcy chose the fourth Sunday in Lent, *Laetare* Sunday, the introit of the Mass of which begins, "Rejoice Jerusalem and come together all you that love her. Rejoice with joy you who have been in sorrow."[55] In 1291 the archbishop of York, employing Dominicans and Franciscans from thirteen communities, organized preaching rallies in thirty-seven separate locations, to be held simultaneously on September 14, the Feast of the Exaltation of the Cross.[56]

The site was also carefully chosen and was often out of doors to achieve maximum effect. Urban II's proclamation of war was made in a field outside Clermont at the end of November; he repeated it, again out of doors, on the banks of the Loire in the following March.[57] Bernard of Clairvaux preached the cross in the open air fifty years later,[58] as did Pope Innocent III seventy years after that.[59] There was a liberal use of visual aids. In 1096 the wandering preacher Peter the Hermit displayed a letter he claimed had been sent to him from heaven.[60] A century and a half later the Master of Hungary, the demagogue who inspired the Crusade of the Shepherds, carried a letter he claimed had been given to him by the Blessed Virgin Mary.[61] In 1146 Bernard of Clairvaux persuaded the king of France, who had taken the cross privately, to appear wearing his cross on a dais beside him and to stand there as a celebrity recruit listening to his address.[62] It was reported in Syria in the 1190s that preachers in Europe stood before a huge canvas screen on which were painted Muslims on horseback desecrating the Holy Sepulchre.[63]

The day of the set-piece sermon would begin with Mass being sung in the presence of as many senior ecclesiastics from the region as could be collected together. In Frisia in June 1214, Oliver of Cologne assembled abbots and priors from local Cistercian, Premon-

stratensian, and Cluniac communities.[64] Then any papal general letter in which Christians were summoned to crusade would be read in
translation. This explains the highly emotional words with which so
many of these letters opened.

> On hearing with what severe and terrible judgement the land of
> Jerusalem has been smitten by the divine hand, we and our broth-
> ers have been confounded by such great horror and affected by
> such great sorrow that we could not easily decide what to do or
> say; over this situation the psalmist laments and says: *O God, the
> heathen have come into thy inheritance.* (Ps. 78 [79]) [Pope Gregory
> VIII, October–November 1187].[65]

The preacher would then launch into his homily. It was common
for this to be quite short and to be based at least partly on the general
letter that had just been read. It would conclude with an *invitatio*, in
which the preacher would implore his listeners to take the cross. In a
handbook for preachers, written in the 1260s, Humbert of Romans
provided twenty-nine examples of *invitationes*. Here is one:

> And so it is clear, most beloved, that those who join the army of
> the Lord will be blessed by the Lord. They will have the angels as
> companions and they will receive eternal rewards when they
> die.[66]

Each of the *invitationes* on Humbert's list ends with the word *cantus*.
Humbert explained in his introduction that an *invitatio* should be accompanied by a hymn. He referred to the *Veni Sancte Spiritus*, the *Veni
Creator*, the *Vexilla regis*, and the *Salve crux sancta*, but he added that the
preacher could arrange for the singing of any other that he deemed
to be suitable.[67] As early as 1100 the archbishop of Milan made use of
a popular song, *Ultreia, ultreia*.[68] So as a preacher bellowed out his passionate appeal a choir would strike up and would presumably con-
tinue singing as men came forward to commit themselves publicly.
   As each recruit made his vow he was presented with a cloth cross.
He was supposed to have it attached to his clothes at once and to wear

this very visible sign of his commitment until he came home with his vow fulfilled.[69] This aspect of the proceedings needed careful preparation, because otherwise there would have been confusion; at Vézelay in 1146 so great was the enthusiasm that the stock of made-up crosses ran out and Bernard of Clairvaux, with typical theatricality, had to tear his habit into strips to provide additional ones.[70] In 1463 Cardinal Bessarion issued the following instruction to preachers: "This is how the cross should be fixed. The attachment should take the same form in all . . . places and should be performed as quickly as possible. When a sign has been made from red silk or cloth, they should attach it to the breast with a pin. Those receiving it may afterwards sew it firmly in place."[71]

A number of thirteenth-century model sermons have survived, because the homilies of admired preachers provided teaching aids at a time when the provision of regular preaching had become a desideratum. They show signs of being honed for wider use,[72] but the fact that they were worked up adds to their value, because they reveal the themes which in the considered judgment of experienced preachers needed to be stressed. I have looked closely at twenty-seven of them, composed between 1213 and 1283.[73] They were written by very distinguished churchmen. James of Vitry, John of Abbeville, and Eudes of Châteauroux ended up as cardinals and papal legates. Humbert of Romans, who was master general of the Dominicans, and Gilbert of Tournai, who was regent master of the Franciscan house in Paris, were leading mendicants. Philip the Chancellor was a well-known theologian and Roger of Salisbury was a bishop. I have supplemented the evidence provided by the sermons with the material in Humbert's own treatises of advice on the preaching of the cross.[74]

The present archbishop of Canterbury has recently asserted that "there is a good deal of reservation [relating to the employment of force] in Christian tradition."[75] But it is certain that if the idea of fighting as a penance—a far more radical idea than that of warfare in the service of God, as we have seen—had worried audiences in the thirteenth century, the preachers would have justified it at length. Nowhere in the material can one find any attempt to do so. Penitential warfare was not brushed under the carpet; on the contrary, the preachers reveled in it. For them, a crusade was a superlative kind of pilgrimage precisely because of the severity of the penance involved.

There is a pilgrimage which is excellent beyond others, namely that of the crusaders, which surpasses other Christian pilgrimages in many ways. For other pilgrimages are made on account of some saint, but this one is made especially on account of the saint of saints, namely Christ. On others people expose themselves to intensive labour, but on this one they expose themselves to death, and this occurs in many instances. Men quickly return from others to their home and fatherland, but on this one they travel far on a long pilgrimage. By this pilgrimage the common good of Christianity is assisted; by the others only personal well-being. Other pilgrims are not given an indulgence, but these ones are given a plenary indulgence of their sins. In these pilgrims the example of Christ, who went to Calvary carrying his own cross, shines forth clearly. So these pilgrims, following Christ, carry his cross, which others do not, as they wear other symbols of pilgrimage. It must be noted that just as this pilgrimage is of a greater standing, so these pilgrims must take greater care to make it in a due and worthy manner.[76]

The tribulations and torments of crusading were stressed over and over again: "Those who take the cross deny, that is to say renounce, themselves by exposing themselves to mortal danger, leaving behind their loved ones, using up their goods, carrying their cross, so that afterwards they may be carried to heaven by the cross."[77] "What greater almsgiving can there be than offering oneself and one's belongings to God and risking one's life for Christ, leaving behind one's wife, children, relations and birthplace for the service of Christ, exposing oneself to dangers on land, dangers at sea, dangers from thieves, dangers from plunderers, the danger of battle for the love of the Crucified?"[78]

The journey into a perilous and alien environment was portrayed as evidence of the love that burned in crusaders, who had emptied their hearts through true penitence.[79] "It is a sign that a man loves God, when he casts aside the world. It is a sure sign that he burns with love for God and with zeal when for God's sake he leaves his fatherland, possessions, houses, sons and wife to go across the sea in the service of Jesus Christ."[80] Audiences were also reminded of the horrors of the sea voyage. "Because of me you [Christ] had your feet fixed on the cross; because of you I have been on a ship amidst a throng of pilgrims and was so cramped that I could not stretch out my feet. Because of me you once drank spoiled wine on the cross; because of you, I drank putrid water swarming with worms for many days on the ship."[81]

The Gospel precept *If any man would come after me, let him deny himself and take up his cross and follow me* (Matthew 16:24 or Luke 14:27) had been associated with the crusade vow by Pope Urban II.[82] For the first eighty years of the movement, however, the image of the cross appears to have been less significant in the words of preachers and the minds of crusaders (in so far as one can see into them) than the reality of the Holy Sepulchre. It was around 1200 that cross-centered language came into its own and in the thirteenth century it was pervasive. For Eudes of Châteauroux, "The cross is the sword with which the Lord fought the earthly powers and their followers and up to now he has not ceased fighting them. . . . And today, who but the knights more aptly and more evidently trust that Christ is their lord. They follow his call and form his army."[83]

More commonly the cross was a badge of penance and a call to imitate Christ. To Humbert of Romans it was the sign of man's redemption, which distinguished Christians from Muslims and marked the crusader's dedication to the service of Christ and his commitment to some share in the Passion. "It is just that we wear [Christ's] cross on our shoulders because of him, having it not only in our heart through faith and in our mouth through confession, but also in our body through the endurance of pain."[84] Roger of Salisbury developed this idea: "We bear the cross when we feel for our neighbours in their infirmities. . . . We bear the cross through the mortification of the flesh. . . . Whoever ascends the [penitential] cross should take care not to come down from it."[85]

That the cross gave meaning to everything was a reflection of the devotional life of the central Middle Ages, which was characterized by an emphasis on the Crucifixion and by the prevalence of affective imagery relating to it, although the loss of the famous relic of the

True Cross at the Battle of Hattin in 1187, about which Latin Christendom became for a time obsessive, and growing Christian pessimism about the recovery of Jerusalem may have contributed as well. "The cross [preached James of Vitry] is the last plank of wood for a shipwrecked world, the wood of life, the scales of justice, the royal sceptre, the diadem of kings, the imperial throne, the shady tree, the rod of punishment, the supporting staff, the banner made red by the blood of Christ, by the sight of which we are encouraged to fight."[86] It was a public manifestation of the crusader's inner conversion.[87]

An example of how widely the crusade had come to be seen as a model penitential exercise is a Lenten sermon preached on March 28, 1283, to an English community of Benedictine nuns at Elstow, near Bedford. The preacher was probably a Dominican. His audience would, of course, never become crusaders, but he used crusade imagery, particularly that relating to the cross, to develop the theme that those who "assumed the cross of penitence" during Lent were themselves true pilgrims, seeking the heavenly kingdom and eternal life with God.[88]

The fact that crusade preachers made the penitential miseries of a crusade an inspiration to recruitment is one reason among many for doubting whether material considerations played much of a part in the motivation of crusaders, at least for expeditions to the East. There is some truth in the association of crusading, taken as a whole, with what might rather anachronistically be called proto-colonialism. The preservation in Christian hands of the kingdom of Jerusalem and the other Levantine settlements had required the exploitation of land and of commerce by colonists and traders.[89] By-products of the crusading movement, such as the Venetian Crete and Genoese Chios, fitted into a classic colonial mold.[90] The occupation of the Baltic seaboard by German, Danish, and Swedish crusaders had colonial features[91] and associations with early imperialism are also to be found in the journeys of exploration patronized by the Portuguese and Castilian kings two hundred years later. The knights of some semisecularized Iberian military orders, particularly those of Santiago and Christ, played major roles in the management of the Portuguese empire.[92] But whether these examples provide firm enough foundations for the generalizations that have been built upon them is open to question, particularly as no economic history of crusading or judgment on its economic effects has ever been written.[93]

The vast majority of crusaders to the East would anyway have considered the prospect of material gain to have been ridiculous. The campaigns were dangerous: recent studies of the First and Fifth Crusades estimate a death rate among the nobles and knights of around 35 percent and casualties would have been higher among the less well-off.[94] They were inconvenient, for both the crusaders and their families. They were always very expensive, with few rewards for the participants, who tended to return home as soon as they were over, and the costs were always causes for concern for them and for their kindred, who as early as the First Crusade were adopting strategies designed to prevent the disposal through sale or pledge of land to which they had good title.[95] Crusading became more and more of a financial burden as the expenses associated with warfare increased and it is arguable that had the papacy not introduced the taxation of the church and the subsidization of crusaders from 1199 onward, the movement would have collapsed through lack of funds. As it was it remained a severe drain on family resources throughout its history.

One cannot identify the point at which the notion of penitential violence began to lose its potency, although more work in the archives of those military orders which survived as orders of the church, the Hospital of St. John on Malta and the Teutonic Order at Mergentheim, may provide an answer. A clue may also be found in the orders' architecture. The exuberant Renaissance flamboyance that transformed the clear simple lines of Tomar into a kind of fairy castle must reflect the fact that the Order of Christ was being secularized and was becoming rich from its management of the Portuguese empire.[96] The architecture of the Knights Hospitaller on Malta was originally as austere as it had been on Rhodes, but in the later seventeenth century decorative fantasies—the work above all of Matteo Preti—began to soften the simple lines and cover the bare walls of the interior of their conventual church in Valletta, while the armorial tradition was carried to extremes in the carpeting of the floor with armigerous mosaic memorials.[97] When the auberge of Castile in Valletta was rebuilt in florid baroque in the eighteenth century, the brother knights, however able and interesting some of them were as individuals, may already have been subconsciously reflecting the reality that their old role and the ethos that underpinned it were becoming anachronistic.

From our point of view, however, penance had been entrenched in and had defined crusading thought and practice for many centuries. Most devout Christians believed that war against those perceived to be the enemies of Christendom and the church was both necessary and beneficial, not only to the religion in general, in that it expressed the will of God, but also to the crusaders, because by taking part they could repay the debt their sinfulness had incurred.

Those who portray the Crusades, in the words of the archbishop of Canterbury to which I referred in the introduction, as "serious betrayals of many of the central beliefs of the Christian faith" must be assuming, as I have already pointed out, not only that warfare of this type is theologically unjustifiable but also that the crusaders were departing from some norm in Christian history. Patently they were not. We might find this uncomfortable aspect of our past easier to confront if we had not arbitrarily confined it to a distant past, airbrushing it so effectively from postmedieval history that we have forgotten how recently it can be identified. In the next chapter I will describe what happened to the crusading movement in the nineteenth century, and toward the end of the book I will try to answer why recent manifestations of it have been so comprehensively wiped from our minds.

CHAPTER THREE

Crusading and Imperialism

On June 2, 1879, Archbishop Lavigerie of Algiers, gravely concerned by the dangers Catholic missionaries were facing in eastern central Africa, suggested to Cardinal Simeoni, the prefect of the Congregation for the Propagation of the Faith, that it might be possible to "restore, under a new form, elements of the old military orders of chivalry, who rendered such great service to the Church in barbarous times and in similar circumstances."[1]

Charles-Martial Allemand-Lavigerie, who had founded the missionary orders of the White Fathers and the White Sisters in 1868 and 1869, was one of the most influential figures in the European missionary field.[2] He had been born in 1825 into a secular bourgeois household, with traditions of freemasonry and support for the French Revolution; his father had refused to fund his seminary education. Nevertheless, his career had been spectacular. He was a professor at the Sorbonne at the age of twenty-eight, bishop of Nancy at thirty-eight, and archbishop of Algiers at forty-two. He was to be a cardinal from 1882 until his death ten years later.

At the age of twenty-two he was appointed director of the *Oeuvre des Ecoles d'Orient*, an agency responsible for raising money to support

French religious communities in the Levant at a time when the Catholics there, particularly the Maronites in Lebanon, were coming under severe pressure. He had visited Lebanon and Syria in 1860 and had become so fired with enthusiasm that in 1872 he unsuccessfully applied to become Latin patriarch of Jerusalem. In 1877 he acquired for his missionaries the beautiful twelfth-century crusader church of St. Anne in Jerusalem, which the French government had bought and restored. This was when French crusade scholarship was in its golden age: no historian today can ignore the works of the Mas Latrie brothers, Rey, Riant, Vogüé, Delaborde, and Delaville le Roulx, or the publications patronized by the *Société de l'Orient latin*. Lavigerie's experiences in the Levant must have aroused in him an interest in the crusade ideal.

Four issues in particular weighed on his mind. The first was the slave trade. Certain that in the end Africa could only be converted to Christianity by its own people and that success was dependent on the suppression of slavery, he became obsessed with its evils. The second was the safety of his missionaries, who were working in a very unstable environment and needed armed protection.[3] The third was an unquestioning commitment to the French cause in the "Scramble for Africa," the race by the European powers to establish suzerainty over the African continent, as each nation tried to seize more than its rivals. The fourth was his fear of competition from "Protestants and Freethinkers," whom, he believed, were penetrating the continent in the wake of the Belgian advance up the River Congo. By the late 1870s he had become convinced that an indigenous Catholic kingdom should be established in eastern central Africa, as a haven for escaped slaves, a center of evangelization, and a barrier to Belgium's eastward expansion.

In May 1883 Father Guillet, the superior of the White Fathers' mission west of Lake Tanganyika, proposed that they should replace the mercenaries whom they regularly employed in their defense with "*frères auxiliaires*, that is to say brothers who, having manual work as their primary and daily occupation, can also train the 'children' [by which he meant his converts] in weaponry, so that they can police the village, and take up arms and fight off brigands in case of attack."

Pointing out that auxiliary brothers of this kind would be more useful than mercenaries, who served relatively short terms, and that they would cost nothing, he asked whether it would be possible to form them into a "sort of Society at the same time religious and militant."[4] Lavigerie, who must have been involved in this proposal, asked the council of the White Fathers to examine whether "one could have two orders of brothers, of which one would bear arms like the old Knights of Malta [as the Knights Hospitaller of St. John were now known], and the other would follow the actual rule of the [White Fathers]; but both would make perpetual vows."[5] When the council discussed this suggestion, a minority was worried that the use of arms in such a manner would compromise the mission, but most were in favor and asked the region's vicar general, Bishop Léonce Bridoux, to look into the rules of various orders, including the old military ones.

In his report Bridoux proposed that brothers-at-arms should accompany the missionaries with special responsibility to defend them and, under the missionaries' direction, to police any new Christian center that could provide a nucleus for a Catholic African kingdom. As professed religious, subject to the superiors of the White Fathers, they were to vow perpetual celibacy, poverty, obedience, and "to consecrate their life to the service and defense of the missions," for which they should be ready to die.[6] Parallels with the establishment in 1158 of the Military Order of Calatrava under the aegis of the Cistercian abbot of Fitero spring to mind.[7]

Lavigerie was worried, however, by the prospect of the Superior of the White Fathers becoming a military commander-in-chief; he pointed out that the old military orders had been run by their brother knights, not by their priests.[8] His mind turned to the possibility of using the Order of Malta (the old Order of the Hospital of St. John) itself. The order had been gradually reviving since the abandonment of its island state, and in 1879 Pope Leo XIII had restored the right, which it had lost in 1805, to have an elected grand master. In his brief the pope had referred to its "surpassing merits in the Church, distinguished by the glory of its history and the victory won against the common enemy."[9] It was now refocusing its efforts on the care of the sick, but Lavigerie saw this as an opportunity to revive its ancient military traditions. In a note addressed to Holy See in June 1884, he returned to his idea of the establishment of a Catholic state in eastern central Africa, which would be a bulwark against Protestant advance, arguing that the reconstituted Order of Malta could be employed to make this a reality. He estimated that the order would have to spend around five hundred thousand francs on a novitiate in Europe and on work in the field.[10]

In effect, he was proposing the establishment of a new order-state west of Lake Tanganyika, along the lines of Prussia and Rhodes in the Middle Ages and of Malta before 1798. He reported that Pope Leo "was personally enthusiastic (the word enthusiastic is not too strong)," but a meeting he had with Grand Master Ceschi of the Order of Malta was a disappointment. The grand master, who probably believed that his order had definitively abandoned a military role and who must have been worried by the prospect of a revival in Africa of the Thirty Years' War, replied that he did not have the resources for such a task. Lavigerie later wrote that he regretted he could not "galvanize those paralytics."[11]

Four years later, in May 1888, he and some of his Algerian diocesans, accompanied by a few African converts, came to Rome on pilgrimage to celebrate the fiftieth anniversary of the pope's ordination to the priesthood. Leo delivered some "verbal instructions," which were not formally recorded, but in which, according to Lavigerie, he "summoned the Christian world to a crusade to end such great horrors [as the commerce in slaves]." Lavigerie presented himself as having been charged to preach this crusade in the pope's name.[12] Speaking in the church of St. Sulpice in Paris on July 1, he called again for an *Association militaire et religieuse*, such as had been created in the past to defend Christians against the Turks, and he claimed somewhat optimistically that the recruitment of five hundred determined and generous young men, who could officer African troops, would be sufficient.[13] His audience thought he had in mind the Order of Malta, which, it was assumed, the pope was reorganizing so that it could involve itself in the work of the redemption of slaves in Africa. Earlier that year on June 12, Leo had restored the rank of cardinal to the grand master and had again written in praise of the order's crusading history "celebrated for its ancient origins, for the virtue and nobility of the brother knights, for their glorious service on behalf of Christianity and the Catholic Faith and for the victories won by them against the enemy of the Christian name."[14] But Lavigerie had washed his hands of the Order of Malta, which was now, he wrote, "only a shadow of its former self."[15] He was again thinking of a new one, with a rule suited to its purpose and its members bound by temporary vows, which would be open to young Christians from various European countries and would be independent of the missionaries.

His proposal was enthusiastically supported by sections of the French public. There was a well-backed appeal for funds to buy the Mediterranean island of Porquerolles (offshore of Hyères) as a base. Laypeople in Lyons put two houses at the disposal of the future militia. Volunteers began to come forward.[16] Interest was also expressed in England and on July 31 Lavigerie addressed a crowded meeting, arranged by the Anti-Slavery Society, in the Prince's Hall in Piccadilly in London. In the presence of Cardinal Manning, the distinguished explorer Verney Cameron, and Charles Smythies, the Anglican bishop of the Universities' Mission to Central Africa, he called for an armed force similar to those that had existed in the Middle Ages. This was too much for most of his listeners, however, and the meeting declared that only governments should resort to arms.[17] One senses that this, the third project Lavigerie had floated, was beginning to run out of steam and the final blow was administered by the avaricious King Leopold II of Belgium, who was planning to take over the "crusade" himself and to absorb it. A meeting between Lavigerie and the king at Ostend on August 10 got nowhere and by the time Lavigerie addressed a conference in Brussels on August 15, the idea of a military order had been abandoned in favor of a secular force that could be rapidly formed.[18]

Within six months, however, Lavigerie was at it again, this time concentrating his efforts in the Algerian desert, now that an agreement with Britain, which on August 5, 1890, would give France almost the whole of northwest Africa as a sphere of influence, was on the horizon. He conceived of fortified asylums in the Sahara, placed on great communication routes and having the additional purpose of "advancing commerce and civilization." These, he wrote in March 1889, could be established by an association "somewhat like the Or-

der of Malta," the members of which would be "volunteers of civilization and peace." In 1890 he began to plan the foundation of this new
order, to be called *L'Institut Religieux et Militaire des Frères Armés du Sahara*.
He had bought an agricultural property at Biskra on the edge of the
desert with money provided by the French antislavery society and
had built there a residence for fifty persons. This was to be the order's
mother house.[19] According to the rule he composed, the *Frères Armés*
were to operate throughout the African desert belt where the indigenous were victims of the slave trade. The brothers would receive escaped slaves, offer hospitality to travelers, work the soil, and befriend
the locals. Lavigerie detailed exactly how their settlements were to be
established. In each of them there was to be a commandant, two lieu-
tenants—one in charge of agriculture, the other of military exercises—and two almoners. Each community was to have a hospital to
care for sick Africans.

The first responsibility of every brother was to be his own sancti-
fication. As penitents and professed religious, subject to the pope
through the vicar apostolic, he and his brethren were to lead "Christian lives, even heroic ones," of "devotion and apostolic charity, work,
self-denial, prayer, zeal, and sanctity." They had to adhere more
strictly than other religious, Lavigerie wrote, to the practice of apostolic poverty. Minutely detailed instructions determined their way of
life, with the aim of corresponding it as closely as possible to that of
the natives among whom they would dwell. They were to live, sleep,
and eat in the manner of the indigenous and had to learn Arabic and
African languages. Their days were to be divided between prayer and
spiritual reading, agricultural work in their settlements, and military
exercises. There were to be regular retreats and frequent confession
and communion.

No postulant was to be less than thirty-five years old unless a special
dispensation had been obtained from the vicar apostolic. Postulancy
would last three months, to be followed by a novitiate of one year.
Vows would then be made for five years, after which they could be
renewed. After ten years the vows would be perpetual. The brothers
were to promise to be obedient to their superiors, to be poor, to be
chaste, "and to fight to death, if it should be necessary, for the defence
and protection of those, principally the victims of slavery, who will

put themselves under this Institute's protection." The brothers had, therefore, to carry arms and know how to use them, and in each settlement they had to build a redoubt and keep an arsenal of weapons.[20]

Hundreds of men from all social classes applied to join the new order and ninety-five were accepted, although the community at Biskra never had more than thirty members. On April 5, 1891, the first brothers received their habits of white emblazoned with a red cross. A daughter community of six brothers was founded at Ouargla, further south, at the end of 1891, and Lavigerie wanted other settlements established even deeper into the interior, but the newspapers, even the Catholic ones, were indifferent or hostile, and the French government became concerned. The order was anyway not developing as he had hoped and the entrants were not of the caliber to provide experienced leaders. Lavigerie, who was now gravely ill—he was to die a week later—took the decision to wind the *Frères Armés* up and sent one of the missionaries to Biskra to break the news on November 19, 1892. The community at that time consisted of twenty-three members. Nine joined the White Fathers, one entered the Trappists, two became colonists, and the others returned home.[21]

The *Institut des Frères Armés* was of course an anachronism. It was a reflection of a reactionary and romantic streak in the French Church as it reeled under assault from anticlerical forces and tried to rediscover its roots in its medieval past. The most famous survivor of the Crusades, the Order of Malta, which had abandoned its military functions and revitalized its ancient mission of mercy, had shown itself to be more pragmatic than Lavigerie. The achievements of its government from 1834 onward in preserving its claims to sovereignty, persuading its members to renounce the role they had followed for seven centuries, readopting the care of the sick as its principal activity, and rebuilding its provincial structure on a new basis, demonstrate how adaptable it was and explain why the grand master was so reluctant to get involved in the creation of an African order-state.[22]

But Lavigerie was not some utopian fantasist. He was a major figure in the process of reconciling the Catholic Church with the French Republic and in its defense against anticlerical onslaught. He was close to the popes and, as we have seen, he founded two of the most successful missionary orders of all time. At least one prominent newspaper believed that he would have made a great pope.[23] His crusade plans attracted support from many people, including Pope Leo XIII, who on hearing of his death was said to have exclaimed: "I loved him as a brother, as Peter loved Andrew."[24] In his interests and political influence Lavigerie reminds one, although obviously on a lesser scale, of the twelfth-century Cistercian abbot Bernard of Clairvaux.

There can be no doubt that he had been engaged in a series of authentic crusade projects. Earlier in this book I drew attention to those elements that were unchanging features of crusading: warfare that was believed to be at the same time holy and penitential; papal authority; the wearing of crosses; and vows, which for the brothers of the military orders were of religious profession. Lavigerie had wanted the Order of Malta to revert to a military role and to create a new order-state. When he could not persuade it to do so, he founded an order of his own, which was to be engaged in both holy and penitential combat and was subject to the papacy. His *Frères Armés*, as professed fighting religious wearing crosses, were not unlike those established in the thirteenth-century Baltic region, where crusades were being fought in defense of missions.[25]

I also commented on the way other aspects of crusading were subject to alteration and development as the movement adapted to new situations and fashions. Lavigerie's ideas were at the same time authentically crusading and the products of nineteenth-century imperialism. His early projects related to French ambitions in eastern central Africa, before they collapsed in the face of the Belgian advance to Lake Tanganyika and the British occupation of Uganda, following the barbarous treatment of Christian converts by the Kabaka Mwanga of Buganda and violence between Catholic and Protestant missionaries. The *Institut des Frères Armés*, on the other hand, was founded to take advantage of the French acquisition of most of the northwestern quarter of the continent.[26]

∼≋≫

His dream of a military order operating in Africa should also be viewed against a background filled with a number of other ventures and obscured by swirling clouds of rhetoric. The schemes and the tone of the language were often as imperialist as they were crusading, but they would still have astonished the heroes of the Enlightenment, who had been in their graves for less than a century and a half. Voltaire and Diderot in France, Hume and Robertson in Scotland, and Gibbon in England had subjected crusading to severe moral criticism and sometimes to derision, even if their opinions were less absolute than is often supposed.[27] The moribund state of crusading had been summed up by Napoleon in his judgment on the defense of Malta by the Knights Hospitaller in 1798: "If the fortifications, the material means of resistance, were immense, the moral resources nullified them."[28] And any remaining case for the Crusades had been undermined by the grisly spectacle of Cardinal Ruffo's undisciplined Christian Army of the Holy Faith rampaging through southern Italy in 1799, committing atrocities in support of the exiled Bourbon king of Naples.[29]

But although disapproval continued to be expressed in the early nineteenth century and Enlightenment distaste was enshrined in popular imagination by Sir Walter Scott's novels (to which I will turn later), a more positive approach to the history of the Crusades began to emerge, fuelled by the prospects of European expansion to the East, the potential benefits of which were revealed by Napoleon's invasion of Egypt, and by a growing appreciation of the Middle Ages.[30]

There is, moreover, nothing like apparent extinction to generate romantic attachment. This was expressed most vividly by Joseph-François Michaud, whose epic *Histoire des croisades* appeared between 1812 and 1822 and was a *succès d'estime*, going through four editions under the French Restoration and a further five under the July Monarchy. A fervent royalist, Michaud believed that crusading had enriched all the European nations engaged in it: "Names made famous by this war are still today objects of pride to families and country. The most positive of the results of the First Crusade is the glory of our fathers, this glory which is also a real benefit for a nation."[31] He went further and maintained that of all European countries, France had benefited the most: "France would one day become the model and centre of European civilization. The holy wars contributed much to this happy development and one can perceive this from the First Crusade onwards."[32]

The patriotic fervor his *Histoire* generated found expression in the *Salles des Croisades* in the Château of Versailles, which King Louis Philippe planned to become a museum dedicated to the glories of France. The five rooms were hung with over 120 paintings, the most famous of which is Eugène Delacroix's *Entry of the Crusaders into Constantinople on the Fourth Crusade*, and were decorated with the coats-of-arms of families whose ancestors had been crusaders. There was fierce competition among French nobles to be included and for years after the rooms opened in 1843 those who had not originally been represented continued to bombard the authorities with demands for inclusion, producing in support of their case documents, many of them forged, attesting to crusading ancestry.[33]

Many other countries developed their own myths of national crusading history. The invented state of Belgium adopted Godfrey of Bouillon.[34] Norwegian nationalists looked to King Sigurd.[35] Germany had eight crusading rulers, above all Frederick Barbarossa.[36] Spain had the glories of the Reconquest, a national war of liberation fought against the Moors, with heroes like St. Ferdinand III of Castile.[37] England—where, in 1876, feelings were running so high over the Ottomans' treatment of the Bulgarians that the author of a pamphlet written for English Catholics had to explain why a crusade could not be launched against the Turks—had Richard Coeur de Lion.[38]

It is therefore not surprising that there were in the nineteenth century a number of what one might call paracrusading projects and much pseudocrusading language. Paracrusading had within it some elements drawn from the old movement, although chosen selectively and distorted. Pseudocrusading had no correspondence to the old reality, but borrowed its rhetoric and imagery to describe ventures—particularly imperialist ones—that had nothing at all to do with the Crusades, as nations already expressing pride in their crusading past became involved in the scramble for empire.

The most striking, and in the long run the most influential, paracrusading enterprise took root in England.[39] In the 1820s the Order of Malta, which had not yet reconciled itself to its loss of its order-state and still hankered after a religio-military role, was in a state of anarchy. The Spanish, German, and Austrian Knights of Malta tended to go their own ways, while the French Knights had arrogated to themselves the right to manage the order's affairs as a whole through a capitular commission, the powers of which they claimed, through a mistranslation of a papal letter, to have been recognized by the pope. They were supported by the French government and, somewhat ambiguously, by the lieutenant grand master, now resident in Italy.[40] But with the capitular commission's head, the Commander Jean-Louis de Dienne, a very old man—it was later said that he was "in his dotage"[41]—power fell into the hands of the chancellor, the Marquis Pierre-Hippolyte de Sainte-Croix-Molay, whose title was doubtful, but was said to be Spanish and to have once been secretary to the chancery of the Spanish and Portuguese Knights. Sainte-Croix was rumored to be deeply in debt and it was later said that he raised in France some thousands of francs with which he decamped.[42] He was, in other words, one of those demimonde French Restoration figures who flit in and out of the pages of *The Count of Monte Cristo*.

With Sainte-Croix in charge, the French Knights of Malta pursued a heady foreign policy with the aim of restoring their order's presence in the Mediterranean. Early nineteenth-century imperialist dreams were being fuelled by the gradual disintegration of the ramshackle Turkish empire and a stage in that process was the Greek revolt against Ottoman Turkish rule,[43] which was attracting adventurers from all over Europe. In July 1823, the French Knights, apparently with the backing of the government of France, entered into an alliance with a Greek faction under Alexander Mavrokordatos. The Greeks recognized the order's sovereignty over the island of Rhodes, which it had not held since January 1, 1523, and bound themselves to cede two other islands to be stepping stones to its reconquest. In return the order would provide troops and raise a war chest of 10 million francs.[44] Accordingly, an attempt was made in the following November to sell on the London market £640,000 worth of stock, returning 5 percent, through the issuing of five thousand bonds, redeemable after twenty years. In a prospectus the order's existing wealth and its ability to meet any debt was described in highly optimistic terms.[45]

The treaty was opposed in Greece by rival liberators, and the governments of England, Austria, and Russia wrecked it. Meanwhile there were rumors that the money raised in London was being misappropriated. The lieutenant grand master published his disavowal of the scheme, revoked any powers the French Knights might claim to have had, and sent an agent from Italy to reorganize them. The government of France, for its part, withdrew its recognition of knighthoods granted by the French capitular commission, which therefore ceased to have any legal existence, and acknowledged only those specifically authorized by the lieutenant himself.[46]

The decision of the lieutenant and the attitude of the government of France had little effect, however, on the council of the French Knights of Malta, which reconstituted itself under the control of Sainte-Croix, confirming the unlimited powers that it had already conferred on him. It was as committed as ever to the Mediterranean adventure and in June 1826 it decided to give all Christians the opportunity to contribute to the recovery of an island headquarters in the Mediterranean and the restoration of the order's ancient naval role. This was a prelude to another appeal to England and Dienne, and Sainte-Croix authorized two emissaries to open negotiations with a Scot called Donald Currie, who lived in London.[47] One of these emissaries was a man called Philippe de Chastelain, a shady character who at times passed himself off as a count and had to be rescued by Currie from a debtor's prison; he ended his days in the 1870s eking out a living in Scotland as a "Professor of the French Language and Drawing in all its Departments in Edinburgh and Peebles."[48] The French thought that Currie was a Scottish gentleman and the owner of an estate. He was, in fact, an army accoutrement manufacturer who, according to Chastelain, was "of some education, but of a very common appearance." He had become known to the French through his trade, had traveled to France, and had met Sainte-Croix.[49]

The agreement made between Currie and the French representatives was recorded in three *Instruments of Convention*, which were signed in August 1827. Currie was empowered to raise £240,000 by private subscription. With the money he was to employ men and to buy arms, munitions, and vessels for a Mediterranean expedition. A "Gallo-Britannic factory," incorporating a hospital, was to be established to provide a base for merchants in the Levant. Two clauses stipulated that financial subscribers could become members of the

Order of Malta and that all officers commissioned by Currie would also have the right to join it.[50] The *Instruments* were followed by a *Letter of Instruction* to Currie, empowering him to set up a hospital to be served by brothers of the Anglican rite, although the receptions of knights must be in accordance with the order's statutes. Although it is certain that the grand magistry in Italy was never consulted on the matter, this hospital was said to be founded "under the direction of the Lieutenant Grand Master," and because it would need financial help in its formative years, three-quarters of the dues owed by a province of the order to its common treasury were to be retained by the English for the time being.[51]

The scheme to raise an expeditionary force in England made some sense in view of the chaos reigning in the Aegean at the time, the growing economic importance of Great Britain, the huge stocks of war surplus that could be bought cheaply, and the large numbers of unemployed English soldiers and sailors who were drifting about the country in the 1820s. The establishment of a commercial center in the eastern Mediterranean answered to the needs of British merchants after the folding of the *Levant Company* in 1825, and the fact that this was to be a private venture, funded by subscription, made it difficult for governments to intervene. There were precedents for the military orders entering into relationships with Protestants—for a time in the seventeenth century the Teutonic Order had contained Lutherans and Calvinists as well as Catholics,[52] and in the eighteenth century the Bailiwick of Brandenburg, a body of Protestant knights of St. John descending from German Hospitaller commanders who had adopted Lutheranism during the Reformation and had remained in being as a corporation, was nominally reunited to Malta.[53] Nevertheless, this projected assault on the Turks, with the aim of restoring to the heirs of the Knights Hospitaller the island order-state they had ruled from 1309 to 1522, was a paracrusading venture, to be funded and carried out by Protestants, who would be rewarded with admission into a Catholic military order.

It had no effect whatsoever in the eastern Mediterranean region and not much money was raised. A number of Knights Hospitaller were enlisted, however, and in February 1830 Sainte-Croix, who was now dreaming of the establishment of a headquarters for the order in

Algeria, authorized Currie and Chastelain to form a committee to revive an English branch. This committee was not recognized by the lieutenant grand master in Italy, but it was the seed from which grew The Most Venerable Order of St. John, familiar in modern England, because its St. John Ambulance posts can be seen in almost every soccer stadium and race course.[54]

The minds of the new English knights of St. John were awash with the glories of the ancient nobility and gentry. They recognized all the virtues they most cared about in the Order of Malta, of which, in spite of everything, they believed themselves to be members—the name of the reigning lieutenant grand master was always placed at the head of their printed material. One of them, Sir William Hillary—who as equerry to the duke of Sussex had visited Malta in 1797 and had seen the grand master's court in its last days of faded splendor, had raised his own regiment in the Napoleonic Wars, and had founded the Royal National Lifeboat Institution—was obsessed by a plan for the Christian reoccupation of the Holy Land and its government by the Order of Malta.[55] But these English knights of St. John, having little understanding of crusade ideology or of Catholic religious life, simply could not comprehend what religious orders were about. They wanted, for example, to turn the Order of Malta into a pluriform, secularized institution. In their opinion, "The Order could no longer either be Monastic or Celibate. It appeared to the English council however to be extremely desirable that a suitable Edifice as the Chef Lieu of the Order, partaking of the character of a modern Club-House, should be founded . . . in Paris."[56]

Although in 1857 they announced that they would support the order's plans to establish a hospital in Jerusalem,[57] their leader, Sir Richard Broun, who had been the original for Disraeli's fictional "Sir Vavasour Firebrace"[58] and was still dreaming of the recovery of Rhodes, wrote that the hospital "is like a recurrence of the Dark Ages, and savours of monkdom, instead of chivalry. We live in a material age, one of progress and rationality; and the Order of St John must aim at higher things than washing the feet, and healing the sores of the few thousands of persons who may think fit to pay visits to the early scenes of the Christian faith."[59]

The early history of the refounded Order of St. John in England had, of course, as much to do with romantic fantasy as with imperialism. But once it had found its feet, and particularly after it had been recognized in 1888 as an order of the British Crown, it spread throughout the British empire, creating out of ancient and, one would have thought, alien traditions a genuinely popular ambulance movement that attracted thousands of indigenous volunteers.[60] It played a role in empire-building that, if differently expressed, paralleled that of the Portuguese military orders in the fifteenth and sixteenth centuries. It was in this respect a much more successful instrument of imperialism than Lavigerie's projects had ever been.

Pseudocrusading shared with Lavigerie's vision and with paracrusading an association with imperialism. It was rhetoric employed to dress up the imperialist ventures that engaged so many European nations. The French occupation of Algeria in 1830 was compared to Louis IX's descent on Tunis in 1270, and in an abridged edition of Michaud's *Histoire* published in 1838, his collaborator, Jean-Joseph Poujoulat, averred that "the conquest of Algiers in 1830 and our recent expeditions in Africa are nothing other than crusades."[61] Two rooms in King Louis Philippe's museum at Versailles were dedicated to critical moments in the Algerian campaign, and on seeing Horace Vernet's painting of the French assault on Constantine in 1837, a contemporary exclaimed that "We find there again, after an interval of five hundred years, the French nation fertilizing with its blood the burning plains studded with the tents of Islam. These men are the heirs of Charles Martel, Godfrey of Bouillon, Robert Guiscard and Philip Augustus, resuming the unfinished labours of their ancestors. Missionaries and warriors, they every day extend the boundaries of Christendom."[62]

When in the 1860s, during the troubles in the Levant that had so moved Lavigerie, the government of Napoleon III decided to intervene in Lebanon on behalf of the Maronites, there was talk of actually proclaiming a crusade. Napoleon addressed the French troops leaving for the Levant in Michaudist language: "You are leaving for Syria. . . . On that distant soil, rich in great memories . . . you will show yourselves to be the worthy descendants of those heroes who carried the banner of Christ gloriously in that land."[63]

The association of a crusading past with the imperialist present was a feature of the empire-building of other European nations. Spain's invasion of Morocco in the 1850s was described as a crusade[64] and the British link between crusading and imperialism was particularly apparent in Sir Claude Conder's *The Latin Kingdom of Jerusalem*, published in 1897. "The Crusades were no wild raids on Palestine resulting only in misery and destruction. The kingdom of Jerusalem was the model of just and moderate rule, such as we boast to have given to India, under somewhat similar conditions."[65] Conder's publisher, the *Palestine Exploration Fund*, advertised his book by recalling that: "The condition of the Orientals [is] almost the same as that when Europe intervened in the Eastern question in the days of Godfrey of Bouillon and of King Richard Lionheart."[66]

The idea of the crusade as an instrument of imperialism continued to be expressed, and even gained some momentum, after a British army invaded Palestine during the First World War and Britain occupied Palestine and France occupied Syria and Lebanon under mandate from the League of Nations. Although the British commander, General Allenby, who entered Jerusalem on December 11, 1917, never made the remark "today the wars of the crusaders are ended" attributed to him—indeed steps were taken to avoid giving offense, particularly as Muslims were serving with the British forces—the magazine *Punch* published a cartoon entitled "The Last Crusade," which had Richard Coeur de Lion gazing at Jerusalem from a distance with the caption: "At last my dream come true."[67] On arriving in Damascus in 1920, the first French military governor of Syria, General Henri Gouraud, was heard to say, "Behold, Saladin, we have returned."[68] The French Mandate in Syria generated a wave of French historical literature, one theme of which was that the achievements of the crusaders provided the first chapter in a history that had culminated in modern imperialism.[69]

By then, however, the rhetoric was dying away, the romance was tarnished and imperialism was coming to be reviled. From the 1920s onward the Crusades, stripped of their ideology, were being interpreted in social and economic terms by Liberal economic historians,[70] one of whose "most cherished notions" was that the movement constituted a turning point in the history of the European economy, even though, as we have seen, no one had ever researched the economic effects of the Crusades. Inheriting from the imperialists the idea that crusading was an early example of colonialism, the Liberals assumed that such a powerful movement could only have been generated by economic forces.[71] The imperialist vision they unthinkingly adopted, in spite of their growing scorn for empire-building, has been very influential, although no convincing case, based on evidence, for the prevalence of the profit-motive among crusaders to the East has ever been made, as I have already pointed out.

≫

Para- and pseudocrusading were related to Lavigerie's authentic military order, in the sense that all emerged from the same environment and drew on the same romantic and imperialistic emotions. Until now the most recent date anyone has given for the demise of the crusading movement has been 1798, when Malta fell to Napoleon. The question arises whether we should be thinking of extending its history to the collapse of Lavigerie's military order in 1892. A historian like myself, approaching the nineteenth century from the direction of the Middle Ages, is tempted to do so, but I wonder whether the initiative for the events I have described lay rather with imperialism itself. Crusading was moribund, as even the Order of Malta recognized and as the short life of the *Frères Armés du Sahara* demonstrated, but its ideas and images were seized on and exploited as a package to serve the ends of empire. This had consequences for the future and we are now paying a price, because the newly emerging Arab nationalists took nineteenth-century imperialist rhetoric literally. They came to believe that the West, having lost the first round in the Crusades, had embarked on another, and their vision of past and present crusading was inherited by a new generation of Pan-Islamists. I will turn in the final chapter to this unexpected and extraordinary development in crusade historiography.

CHAPTER FOUR

Crusading and Islam

On October 31, 1898, Kaiser Wilhelm II of Germany, engaged in what the Berlin critic Alfred Kerr sardonically described as a "crusade in comfort," made a fool of himself in Jerusalem. Pushing "to its extreme the arabico-medieval fantasy . . . in medieval garb in front with a Lohengrin breastplate and in Arab dress behind," he wore a white uniform of his own design, embellished with a helmet surmounted by a gold eagle, to which he had added "a garment recalling in some measure his character as a pilgrim, a white silk dust dress, so fashioned as to resemble a palmer's cowl." Breaking with convention by entering the city through a specially prepared breach in the walls, he was followed "by a host of knightly figures arrayed in the insignia and flowing mantles of the Order of St John," among whom rode Mr. Thomas Cook Jr., the owner of the tour company that had organized the trip, carrying a banner inscribed *Thomas Cook and Son*. Once inside the city the kaiser, donning the white mantle of a Teutonic Knight, attended the dedication of the Evangelical Lutheran church of the Redeemer, which now overshadowed the church of the Holy Sepulchre nearby. He had also acquired land on Mount Sion on which to erect the equally ostentatious German Catholic abbey of the Dormition and sponsored the building of a German hospice on the Mount of Olives, in the chapel of which he and his wife were portrayed, surrounded by the eight German crusader kings to whom I have already referred.[1]

He traveled on to Damascus where on November 8 he laid a satin flag and a wreath, with an inscription dedicated to "the Hero Sultan Saladin," on Saladin's dilapidated tomb. He was to pay for the restoration of the mausoleum and the construction of a very un-Islamic marble tomb-chest, on which there came to rest another wreath, this time in bronze gilt and inscribed "From one great emperor to another." At a banquet afterward he expressed his delight at treading the same soil as Saladin, "one of the most chivalrous rulers in history," who, he added, had been "a knight *sans peur et sans reproche*, who often had to teach his adversaries the true nature of chivalry."[2]

With this bombastic theater the kaiser reintroduced Saladin to the Muslims, who had almost completely forgotten him. Saladin had been overshadowed in their collective memory both by his predecessor Nur ad-Din, who had encouraged religious reform and had united the local Muslim principalities against the crusaders, and by the Mamluk sultan Baybars, a better general and more effective strategist, who had reigned a century later and had done much to bring the Christian settlements in the Levant to an end. There had been, it is true, signs of a stirring of interest in Saladin. Namik Kemal had published a biography in Turkish in 1872 and a play by Najib Sulayman, based on Sir Walter Scott's *The Talisman*, had been performed in Alexandria in 1895.[3] But the Egyptian poet Ahmad Shawqi could still ask how it was that Saladin's greatness had been ignored by Muslim writers until they had been reminded of it by Kaiser Wilhelm.[4]

Saladin's relative obscurity in Muslim history was understandable. He was a Kurd. He had an attractive, if ruthless, personality, but his commitment to his religion had been doubtful and he had often been in trouble with the caliph in Baghdad. He was shrewd and ambitious, and he had achieved one stunning victory that he had followed up by reoccupying Jerusalem, but he had also allowed the Third Crusade to reconquer much of the Levantine coast and the quasi-empire he built up lasted less than eighty years.[5] In medieval Europe, however, he had gained legendary status as a non-Christian paladin of chivalry. This

Western tradition that influenced, for example, Gotthold Ephraim Lessing's sympathetic portrait of him in his dramatic poem *Nathan the Wise* (1778), was mined by the most popular of the nineteenth-century romantic writers, Sir Walter Scott, who established a more critical, but just as influential, tradition alongside the one that I have already described stemming from Joseph-François Michaud. Indeed, if Kaiser Wilhelm's behavior in Jerusalem had recalled the pseudo-crusading imperialism originating in Michaud, his actions and words in Damascus gave expression to the critical romanticism of Scott, on the works of whom he had been brought up by his English mother.[6]

Four of Scott's novels involved crusades and crusaders. *Count Robert of Paris* (1831) was set in Constantinople at the time of the First Crusade; the other three were set during the Third Crusade. *Ivanhoe* (1819) and *The Betrothed* (1825) were concerned with events on the home front, while the plot of *The Talisman* (1825) was set in Palestine and centered on the friendship between a Scottish knight and Saladin, who appeared in a bewildering array of disguises, including that of a skilled physician who cured King Richard of England. The novels painted a picture of crusaders who were brave and glamorous, but also vainglorious, avaricious, childish, and boorish. Few of them were genuinely moved by religion or the crusade ideal; most had taken the cross out of pride, greed, or ambition. The worst of them were the brothers of the military orders, who may have been courageous and disciplined but were also arrogant, privileged, corrupt, voluptuous, and unprincipled. An additional theme, the cultural superiority of the Muslims, which was only hinted at in the other novels, pervaded *The Talisman*. In his introduction to later editions Scott wrote that "the warlike character of Richard I [of England], wild and generous, a pattern of chivalry, with all its extravagant virtues and its no less absurd errors, was opposed to that of Saladin, in which the Christian and English monarch showed all the cruelty and violence of an Eastern Sultan; and Saladin, on the other hand displayed the deep policy and prudence of a European sovereign."[7]

It was not hard for Scott, as a child of the eighteenth-century Enlightenment influenced by the Scottish historian William Robertson, who had stressed the superiority of Islamic civilization,[8] to portray the crusaders as backward and unenlightened, crudely assailing more civilized and sophisticated Muslims, but his vision of the past was an unreal one. Leaving aside the actual state of cultural development in Western Europe and the Near East in the twelfth century—and they were not nearly as far apart as Scott and his audience supposed—any reading of history that placed the crusaders in one context—the central Middle Ages—and their opponents in another—the nineteenth century—was wholly anachronistic. Under his faux-oriental clothing, Scott's Saladin was patently a modern liberal European gentleman, beside whom medieval Westerners would always have made a poor showing.[9]

The Talisman was Scott's most popular crusade novel after Ivanhoe. It was dramatized on many occasions and was translated into many European languages. It inspired painters in Britain, France, and Italy and its picture of Saladin influenced generations of writers and politicians.[10] William Ewart Gladstone, enraged in 1876 by the atrocities attributed to the Turks in Bulgaria, compared them unfavorably to "the chivalrous Saladins of Syria."[11] Saladin's ruinous tomb in Damascus began to feature on European sightseeing tours—the prince of Wales visited it in 1862[12]—but it took the kaiser's overblown homage to bring him fully to public attention in the Levant.

The potency of Scott's critically romantic approach is demonstrated by the way it continues to suffuse European and American writing on the Crusades, scholarly as well as popular. The most admired history in English, that by Sir Steven Runciman, like Scott a Lowlander, is almost what Scott would have written had he been more knowledgeable. In it the crusaders are characterized as courageous and colorful, but often childish and boorish and never very reflective, and the peroration with which it famously ends could almost have been written by Scott himself: "There was so much courage and so little honour, so much devotion and so little understanding. High ideals were besmirched by cruelty and greed, enterprise and endurance by a blind and narrow self-righteousness; and the Holy War itself was nothing more than a long act of intolerance in the name of God, which is a sin against the Holy Ghost."[13] One reviewer, August Krey, perhaps echoing General Bosquet at the Battle of Balaclava, commented of this rhetoric that it "may be appropriate in rounding out a literary tragedy, but is it history?"[14]

Another example of Scott's enduring influence—this time at the level of Western entertainment—is the film *The Kingdom of Heaven*, released in 2005, throughout which a cruel, avaricious, and cowardly Christian clergy preaches unadulterated hatred against the Muslims. The priests' stupidity and fanaticism is echoed in minds of the crusaders, the Templars, and most of the leaders of the Christian settlement around Jerusalem, which is portrayed as a kind of nineteenth-century America, a "New World" welcoming enterprising immigrants from an impoverished and repressive Europe. In the midst of the zealotry and bigotry a brotherhood of freethinkers has vowed to create an environment in which all religions can coexist in harmony. They are in touch with Saladin, who shares their aims of toleration and peace, but zealots on the Christian side set out to wreck any chance of an accommodation with Islam.

The approach of the critical romantics, from Walter Scott to Ridley Scott, was obviously alien to the romantic imperialistic tradition stemming from Joseph-François Michaud. In Scott's critically romantic version, barbarous and destructive crusaders, morally and culturally inferior, had faced civilized and modern-thinking Muslims. To the romantic imperialists, on the other hand, these same crusaders had brought enlightenment to a heathen world. But with imperial ideology in decay in the early twentieth century, the way was opened for profound changes in the historiographical tradition as the lines descending from Scott and Michaud, from the Enlightenment and imperialism, converged to give birth to a materialistic vision, which inherited from Scott the image of an inferior Western culture barging its way into a more sophisticated region and from Michaud's heirs the belief that the motivation for this had been a protocolonialist one.

In a speech at the banquet that followed his veneration of Saladin's tomb in 1898, the kaiser stated that "the [Turkish] sultan and the three hundred million Muslims who revere him as their leader should know that the German emperor is their friend forever," thus appearing to lend his support to the policies of the Ottoman sultan Abdulhamid II at a time when the Turkish empire was in crisis. Faced with revolt and disintegration in the Balkans and lambasted by the press and politicians in Western Europe, the Ottomans had been forced to recognize the independence of Romania, Serbia and Montenegro, and the autonomy of Bulgaria, and to surrender territories to the Russians, Greeks, French, and British. But even this massive disgorgement had not satisfied their critics.

The response of Sultan Abdulhamid had been to turn to Pan-Islamism, an ideology enshrining the unity of all Muslims under one world authority. He was a pious man who took his role as caliph, the politico-spiritual leader of Sunni Islam, very seriously, particularly as his right to hold the caliphate was being challenged. But he went further. He publicized his conviction that the European imperialists had embarked on a new "crusade." In using this term he was, of course, echoing the rhetoric that had washed round Western Europe for more than half a century. It is even possible that he had heard of Lavigerie's experiment in Algeria. At any rate, Sayyid 'Ali al-Hariri, the author of the first Muslim history of the crusading movement, published in 1899, wrote in his introduction that "Our most glorious sultan, Abdulhamid II, has rightly remarked that Europe is now carrying out a crusade against us in the form of a political campaign."[15]

One often reads that modern Muslims have inherited from their medieval ancestors bitter memories of the violence of the crusaders.[16] Nothing could be further from the truth. The invasion of Syria and Palestine from 1097 to 1099 had indeed come as a shock to a region that had already for fifty years been a theater of war between a resurgent Sunnism, spearheaded by the Selchük Turkish sultanate on behalf of the 'Abbasid caliphate in Baghdad, and the Fatimid caliphate in Cairo, a center of vigorous proselytizing Shi'ism. Both sides, however, had been gravely weakened. In 1092 one of the greatest figures in Selchük history, the vizier Nizam al-Mulk, the power behind the sultans for over thirty years, was murdered. A month later the Selchük sultan Malikshah died in suspicious circumstances. He was followed to the grave not only by his wife, grandson, and other powerful figures, but also by the 'Abbasid Caliph al-Muqtadi himself. With this wipe-out the Selchük sultanate, which stretched from Asia Minor to Iran, disintegrated into principalities in which pretenders and members of the family fought each other for power. In 1094 the Fatimid Caliph al-Mustansir, who had ruled for fifty-eight years, also died. So did his vizier, Badr al-Jamali. Although none of the crusaders knew it, they were marching toward a door that had swung wide open.[17]

After some rather desperate counterattacks, the reaction of most of the petty Muslim states into which the Selchük sultanate had fragmented was to reach a *modus vivendi* with the new settlers. There followed periods of détente during which the Westerners appear to have constituted for most Muslims little more than an irritant, although Arab writers loved to dwell on traditional stereotypes: that they were unhygienic, dull, coarse, sexually lax, gullible, and hypocritical.[18] Nevertheless, there soon began a revival of the idea of *jihad*, which was at first confined to a few religious leaders in Damascus and Aleppo, but came to the surface twenty years after the First Crusade and was vigorously promoted in the enthusiasm that accompanied the first major Muslim reconquests in 1144. It was to be brilliantly exploited by Nur ad-Din after the failure of the Second Crusade in 1149. *Jihad* propaganda was expressed in every possible medium—poetry, letters, treatises, sermons, and inscriptions—and in it two themes stood out: the obligation to reconquer the Levantine coastlands, and especially the city of Jerusalem, from the Christians and the conviction that this could only be achieved through Muslim religious and political unity. Nur ad-Din's successor, Saladin, took up these themes in a propaganda and military campaign that culminated in his reconquest of Jerusalem in 1187.[19]

Jihadist propaganda was less in evidence under Saladin's successors. It was only when they were overthrown in 1250 by their own Mamluks, specially trained slave-soldiers from the frontiers of Islam, that the situation was transformed. Under the new rulers of Egypt, particularly Baybars, there was an upsurge of *jihadism*. Born a Kipchak Turk, Baybars remained very much a Turkish warrior chieftain, but he was a good administrator and a fine general and his methodical approach to the reconquest of the coast made it possible for his successors to drive the Westerners out in 1291.[20]

The works of two Muslim authors provide clear examples of the *jihadist* themes of reconquest and the need for religious reformation, which would lead to the unity necessary if the reconquest was to be successful and lasting. The first, who taught at the beginning of the period of Western settlement, lived before the Syrian *jihad* had got into its stride, but the other, writing at the very end, has had a profound influence on modern Sunni *jihadism*.[21] As-Sulami, a teacher at the great mosque in Damascus, dictated his *kitab al-jihad* over the course of the year 1105. For him, participation in holy war was the responsibility of every able-bodied Muslim, particularly when Islam was under attack. The scandals of disunity and of his coreligionists' neglect of their duty risked divine displeasure, but they were now being given a chance to reconcile themselves to God, since moral reformation was absolutely necessary if the war against the Western invaders was to succeed.[22]

For Ibn Taymiyya, who wrote around 1300, after the collapse of the Western mainland settlements but at a time when there was still a substantial Christian presence in the region, the priority was not to wage war extraliminally in the *dar al-harb*, but to turn inward and purge the Sunni world itself of infidels and heretics. Recognizing that the Jews and Christians who were resident within Islamic borders were to some extent protected, he argued that the goal must nevertheless be the eventual eradication of their imperfect monotheism. This could be achieved, he believed, by the strict enforcement of the *dhimma* regulations applying to their communities, which would make conditions intolerable for them. Meanwhile, in an approach to heresy very similar to that of his Latin Christian contemporaries, he condemned the Shi'ites as interior enemies "even more dangerous than the Jews and the Christians" and he wanted holy war to be waged pitilessly against them. The introspective *jihad* was for him to be a force that at the same time would renew individual spirituality and create a united society dedicated to God which could then triumph over the world.[23]

It was naturally the case that Muslim writers, faced with the need to resist and then expel the Europeans from Palestine and Syria, devoted a good deal of space to their enemies in the twelfth and thirteenth centuries. Crusades and *jihads* continued to be preached, of course, but in the later Middle Ages the focus of interest moved from the Levant to the Balkans, which were being overwhelmed by an Ottoman tide. In the Islamic world the Crusades almost passed out of mind, although, as we have seen, legendary heroes of resistance like Baybars continued to figure in folk memory.[24] Very few writers, apart from the Ottoman historiographer Naʿima, who drew comparisons between the central Middle Ages and the struggle in the Balkans at the turn of the seventeenth and eighteenth centuries, did more than mention the crusaders in passing.[25] It is only a slight exaggeration to say that between 1500 and 1860 the most original writings on the Crusades in Arabic—Christian Maronite histories written in Lebanon—were nostalgic about them.[26]

The fact is that the Muslims had lost interest. They had never shown much concern about the world beyond Islam, since there is a tendency, in the words of one scholar, "to treat the house of war as one." Following a tradition attributed to the Prophet—"unbelief is one nation"—no particular need was felt to differentiate one infidel from another or to distinguish crusading from other forms of Christian warfare.[27] This unconcern with the distinctions to be made between other religions is still sometimes expressed today: "An unbeliever [kafir] is anyone who follows a religion other than Islam. He is neither a believer nor a Muslim. Idolators, Jews, Buddhists, Christians and Communists are exactly the same in this respect—all will be consigned eternally to Hellfire on the Day of Judgement."[28]

And anyway the Muslims looked back on the Crusades with indifference and complacency. In their eyes they had been the outright winners. They had driven the crusaders from the lands they had settled in the Levant and had been triumphant in the Balkans, occupying far more territory in Europe than the Western settlers had ever held in Palestine and Syria. The Ottoman empire, which in the seventeenth century had extended into Hungary, had laid siege to Vienna twice. The first history of the Crusades in Arabic, which had appeared in 1865, had been a Christian one and a specific Arabic term for them had only been introduced in the middle of the nineteenth century by the Christian intelligentsia.[29]

In the 1890s, however, as the Islamic world, provided with the caliph's remark that the Crusades were still in train, showed signs of taking an interest in them, it was presented with the Western constructs that I have already described.[30] In one, culturally inferior crusaders had faced civilized, liberal, and modern-looking Muslims. In the other, these same crusaders were a source of imperialistic pride for their European descendants, who were now returning to complete the work they had begun. It was easy to gloss this with the view that Europe, having lost the first round in the Crusades, had embarked on another and this reading of the present struck a chord in Arab Nationalism, which was beginning to emerge in response to the British and French occupation of much of North Africa and the Levant and the settlement of Jews in Palestine.

From the first approach, stemming from Scott, the Muslims took the idea of a destructive and savage West, which benefited by absorbing their civilized values while at the same time leaving a trail of wreckage in its wake. As one North African historian asked, "Is it possible to imagine any substantial advantage that the Islamic world has drawn from the crusades? Indeed, how could Islam benefit from contacts established with an inferior, backward civilization?"[31] Saladin, now Arabized,[32] was given a heroic status and within fifteen years of the kaiser's visit an Arab author, warning against the threat posed by Zionist settlement in Palestine, had adopted Saladin as a *nom de plume*. A university named after him was opened in Jerusalem in 1915.[33] In the contemporary novelist Mahmoud Darwish's account of the invasion of Lebanon by the Israelis in 1982, their actions, described in much the same terms as those of Scott's crusaders, are compared unfavorably with the courtesy of Saladin. "Our water [in Beirut] has been cut off by those acting on behalf of leftover crusaders, yet Saladin used to send ice and fruits to the enemy."[34]

From the second European approach, stemming from Michaud, Muslim writers took the idea of a continuing Western assault. In 1920 Saladin was praised for thwarting the *first* European attempt to subdue the East.[35] Following a somewhat eccentric view, propounded by René Grousset and publicized in the Islamic world in the 1930s by 'Aziz 'Atiya, that a cultural fault line divides Occident and Orient, the endemic warfare between Christianity and Islam was sometimes put in the context of a global conflict, the origins of which predated the emergence of the religions.[36] Echoes of this can perhaps be seen in the apparent references by Islamist *jihadis* to Samuel Huntington's revival of this theory under a somewhat different form.[37] But, under the influence of the Liberal economic historians to whom I have already referred, the struggle was more commonly believed, rather perversely in view of the Muslim invasions of the seventh century, to have originated with the Crusades themselves, which constituted the first chapter in European colonial expansion and were manifestations of Western colonialist avarice conducted under the mask of religion.[38] As early as 1934 a writer was maintaining that "the west is still waging crusading wars against Islam under the guise of political and economic Imperialism."[39] Others developed the notion that after losing the first round the West was consumed with a spirit of vengeance and a longing to overturn that Muslim victory. The First World War had marked yet another attempt to take the holy city of Jerusalem, while complicity in the creation of the state of Israel, established on the very ground occupied by the Latin kingdom of Jerusalem, had been an act of vengeful malice. Mahmoud Darwish described the Israeli siege of Beirut in 1982 as "revenge for all medieval history."[40] This idea appeals particularly to the Islamists. "The crusaders' malice remained concealed in their hearts, till they disclosed it when they succeeded in doing away with the Ottoman caliphal state and then establishing a Jewish state in Palestine. This they deemed a two-fold revenge for their defeat at the hand of the heroic Muslim leader Saladin."[41]

It is commonly believed that the victory of Islam over the medieval crusaders can be replicated and the successful *jihads* of the twelfth and thirteenth centuries are sometimes presented as models for future action. In his two-volume *History of the Crusades* (1963) the historian Sa'id Ashur wrote that "our condition is very close to that of our ancestors eight and a half centuries ago; it is consequently incumbent upon us to study the movement of the crusades minutely and scientifically."[42] Conditions and events in the past are therefore examined carefully to provide exemplars, as indeed they are from an opposite point of view in Israel, as I have already pointed out.[43]

Many Nationalists considered their struggle for independence to be a predominantly Arab riposte to a crusade that was being waged against them. Since the 1970s, however, they have been challenged by a renewed and militant Pan-Islamism, the adherents of which have globalized the Nationalist interpretation of crusade history, recognizing at the same time that the crusaders were motivated by ideology—the ideology, of course, of Satan—something that the thoroughly secular Nationalists had refused to consider.

The heightened vision of the Islamists owes most to the ideologue Sayyid Qutb (1906–66), who began his career as an Egyptian Nationalist and ended it in 1966 as an Islamist on the gallows. In prison for most of the last twelve years of his life, he wrote there some of his most profound and influential works. Influenced by Ibn Taymiyya, the medieval *jihadist* to whom I have already referred,[44] he rejected all secular and nationalist ideologies, all non-Islamic philosophy and all tribal and regional allegiances. These, he believed, contributed to the spread of *jahiliyah*, an ignorance of, and therefore a failure to subject oneself to, God, which had been prevalent in the pagan world encountered by the earliest Muslims and was undermining Islam today. The only way forward for Muslims—or at first a select group of them—was to sever all ties with the outside world and to devote themselves entirely to following the word of God in the Koran as a prelude to the reestablishment of *'aqidah*, Islam's authentic spirit, which would eventually be expressed in the total unity of the Muslim world. Mustered against *'aqidah* were potent alien, international, and aggressive forces: Zionism, communism, and crusaderism (*sulubbiya*), the last of which was intimately linked to colonialism. Indeed, in the colonialist age "Europe mustered all its forces to extinguish the spirit of Islam, revived the inheritance of the crusaders' hatred and employed all the material and intellectual powers at its disposal."[45] For Qutb, in fact, crusaderism was a much more ancient and potent force than colonialism; indeed it was almost as if it was embedded in European genes. "Western blood," he wrote, "carries the spirit of the crusades within itself. It fills the subconscious of the west."[46]

It is common for his militant successors to view Zionists and Marxists, and now also Hindus, as surrogates of crusaderism, employed to subvert Islam and destroy believers.[47] It is clear that although the eventual aim of the *jihadis* is world Islamic government under a caliph, their present focus is on Islam itself. They are religio-political reformers engaged in the purification of Islam as a prelude to its eventual triumph. This requires them to focus on two battlefields: one on which they face down corrupt internal forces; the other on which they confront outside powers that are penetrative and are potent enough to nullify their work of reconstruction. Justifying their ruthless violence is hatred of the infidel and his values, of course, but also a fear that their religious experiment will founder. They invoke the Crusades over and over again, since it is crusaderism that lies behind and exploits all the forces ranged against them. "For the first time the Crusaders have managed to achieve their historic ambitions and dreams against our Islamic *umma*, gaining control over the Islamic holy places and the Holy Sanctuaries, and hegemony over the wealth and riches of our *umma*."[48] "Ever since God made the Arabian Peninsula flat, created desert in it and surrounded it with seas, it has never suffered such a calamity as these Crusader hordes, that have spread in it like locusts, consuming its wealth and destroying its fertility."[49]

In a recent broadcast, Osama bin Muhammad bin Laden provided a geography of modern countercrusading warfare. It encompasses Iraq, Afghanistan, Kashmir, Pakistan, Palestine, Sudan (the south and the Darfur region), Somalia, Morocco, Bosnia, Chechnya, and East Timor.[50] Afghanistan has been for decades, of course, a theater of this war. "The battle is between Muslims—the people of Islam— and the global Crusaders. . . . The One God, who sustained us with one of his helping Hands and stabilized us to defeat the Soviet Empire, is capable of sustaining us again and allowing us to defeat America on the same land."[51] But now Iraq is the chief battleground.

> Despite the numerous crusader attacks against our Muslim nation in military, economic, cultural, and moral aspects, the gravest of them all is the attack against our religion, our Prophet and our Sharia tenets. The epicentre of these wars is Baghdad, the seat of the rule of the caliphate. . . . Their defeat in Iraq will mean defeat in all their wars and a beginning of the receding of their Zionist-Crusader tide against us.[52]

In a war of civilizations,

> The *umma* is asked to unite itself in the face of the Crusaders' campaign, the strongest, most powerful and most ferocious campaign to fall on the Islamic *umma*. . . . This is a war which, like previous wars, is reviving the Crusades. Richard the Lionheart, Barbarossa from Germany, and Louis from France—the case is

similar today, when they all immediately went forward the day Bush lifted the cross. The Crusader nations went forward. . . . They have accepted the rule of the cross.[53]

It is this vision of a continuing crusade and of resistance to it that has suddenly and spectacularly forced itself on the world outside. The language employed is often feverish, but a Muslim does not have to be an extreme Islamist to hold to the view that the West is still engaged in crusading. I recently refused to take part in a television series, produced by an intelligent and well-educated Egyptian woman, for whom a continuing Western crusade was an article of faith. Having less to do with historical reality than with reactions to imperialism, the Nationalist and Islamist interpretations of crusade history help many people, moderates as well as extremists, to place the exploitation they believe they have suffered in a historical context and to satisfy their feelings of both superiority and humiliation.

There is nothing new about the *jihadism*, of course, but the form of it that has become such a feature of radical Islamism has some unusual characteristics. Globalization and migration has blurred the geographical boundaries between the *dar al-Islam* and the *dar al-harb* and has provided the *jihadists* with the opportunity, denied to their predecessors, to deliver long-range blows. The powers, which a century and a half ago could easily crush local *jihads* proclaimed against them as their authority advanced inexorably across Asia and Africa, are now relatively weak.[54] And, as I have demonstrated, modern *jihadism* has developed and elaborated the perception of a crusading past and present, which it inherited from Arab Nationalism.

It is clear that this potent historical vision has on it the stamp of that nineteenth-century European association of crusading and imperialism that I have already described. And it is notable that in its responses to *jihadi* terrorism the West has not tried to counter the Muslim reading of history, in spite of the fact that it is in many ways a distortion of reality. As coheirs of the traditions that originated in the writings of Scott and Michaud, most Westerners seem to regard crusading in much the same light as the Muslims, with the differences that until recently they were barely conscious of the Muslim conviction that it was still in train and are ashamed of it rather than defiant. In the late 1990s there were calls for the Catholic Church to apologize for the Crusades. There is a general belief that the pope did so, but although there was an expression of contrition for "sins committed in the service of truth" and the papacy later got near to apologizing to the Orthodox Church for the sack of Constantinople in 1204,[55] the order of service for the ceremony in St. Peter's on March 12, 2000, the Day of Pardon, contained no specific reference to the Crusades.[56] In any case, an apology for past events would have been futile as far as the Muslims are concerned, since crusading is for them still a reality, conducted in more sophisticated and effective ways than ever before.

Western society cannot reply effectively, because it does not comprehend or even recognize the sources of the language the Muslims use. Three of my grandparents were living when in 1892 Cardinal Lavigerie closed down his military order, but our society has completely forgotten how recently crusade ideas were intellectually respectable. The short biography of Pope Leo XIII in the third edition of *The Oxford Dictionary of the Christian Church* describes how he tried "to bring the Church to terms with modern civilization" and "the lead he gave on the burning political and social questions of his time," but it contains no reference to the letters of privilege he issued in 1879 and 1888, praising the Knights of Malta "for their glorious service on behalf of Christianity and the Catholic Faith and for the victories won by them against the enemy of the Christian name."[57] Cardinal Lavigerie's entry praises this "passionate and far-sighted man" for his commitment to the Africans and his foundation of the White Fathers and the White Sisters, but is silent about his obsession with crusading.[58]

It is hard to explain this amnesia. Pseudocrusading language was occasionally to be found throughout the twentieth century. It was, for example, employed by the Nationalists during the Spanish Civil War in the 1930s and by General Dwight D. Eisenhower in his account of the Second World War.[59] As often as not, however, it was greeted with derision and it is significant that the South American militants of Christian Liberation in the 1960s never referred back to crusade thought, in spite of the fact that elements in their theology—the use of force in the names of Christ and fraternal charity, and a belief in martyrdom in battle—could class them as paracrusaders.[60] The parallels eluded them, of course, and it may be that in the minds of most people memories of the nineteenth-century projects and hyperbole could not survive the experience of the First World War, to the realities of which pseudocrusading rhetoric provided an almost obscene counterpoint. In an Advent Sermon in 1915, Bishop Winnington-Ingram of London resorted to language that was more extreme than any to be found in genuine crusade propaganda. "Everyone that loves freedom and honour, everyone that puts principle above ease, and life itself beyond mere living, are banded in a great crusade—we cannot deny it—to kill Germans: to kill them not for the sake of killing, but to save the world."[61] Basil Bourchier, a London vicar who was serving as an army chaplain, described the war as "the holiest that has ever been waged. . . . It is the honour of the most high God which is imperilled" and viewed the Dardanelles campaign as "the latest of the crusades. Should Constantinople fall it will be the greatest Christian victory that has occurred for hundreds of years. . . . A vision arises before the mind of Byzantium once again a Christian city; St. Sophia once again the home of Christian worship, and who knows, once again the Holy Land rescued from the defiling grip of the infidel."[62]

The same chauvinistic hysteria was to be heard in Germany, although modified there by the alliance with Turkey, and in France, where it helped fuel the cult of Joan of Arc. It contrasted sharply with most memorialization, which was compassionate and agonizingly sad.[63] The vast majority of churchmen would have agreed with Henry Scott Holland, the Regius Professor of Divinity in Oxford, who compared the language of some of his coreligionists to "mad Mullahs preaching a Jehad"[64] and, although the idea of the First World War as a holy one was sometimes echoed in British village war memorials,[65] the effusions of men like Winnington-Ingram must have had a negative effect on public opinion. It is possible that crusade rhetoric had become so embarrassing and abhorrent that the seriousness with which crusade ideas had been treated by leading figures as recently as the 1890s was consigned to oblivion.

Conclusion

I have traveled from the eleventh century to the twenty-first, concentrating on the periods 1095 to 1300 and 1800 to 2007. We are today subjected to religio-political hostility, erupting in acts of extreme violence, and a war of words in the course of which the Crusades feature prominently. We cannot hope to understand the circumstances in which we find ourselves unless we are prepared to face up to fact that modern Western public opinion, Arab Nationalism, and Pan-Islamism all share perceptions of crusading that have more to do with nineteenth-century European imperialism than with actuality.

The Crusades themselves were deeply embedded in popular Catholic ideas and devotional life. They were not thoughtless explosions of barbarism. The theory of force that underlay them was relatively sophisticated and was considered to be theologically justifiable by a society that felt itself to be threatened. It is hard now to conceive of the intensity of the attachment felt for the holy places in Jerusalem, the concern aroused by heresy and physical assaults on the church, and the fear Westerners had of Muslim invaders, who reached central France in the eighth century and Vienna in the sixteenth and again in the seventeenth. The men and women who took the cross seem mostly to have been pious and well-intentioned. When Humbert of Romans, who was trying to answer the point that harm was done to Christendom by the deaths of so many decent men on crusade, answered that "by this kind of death people make their way to heaven who perhaps would never reach it by another road," he was merely stating what nearly all his contemporaries believed.[1]

Humbert's words now sound as if they had been written by someone not from an earlier age but from another planet. But before we become too certain of our rectitude and complacent about how far our society has advanced, we should remember that secular ideological violence—"ethical" in the sense that it is employed on behalf of a religious or cultural or even pseudoscientific ideal that is considered by its adherents to be of universal importance—has manifested itself recently in wars waged in the names of imperialism, nationalism, Marxism, fascism, anticolonialism, humanitarianism, and even liberal democracy.

NOTES

INTRODUCTION

1. See Jonathan Riley-Smith, *What Were the Crusades?*, 3rd ed. (Basingstoke, 2002), xi–xii; Norman Housley, *The Later Crusades, 1274–1580: From Lyons to Alcazar* (Oxford, 1992), 2–6; Norman Housley, *Contesting the Crusades* (Oxford, 2006), 1–23; Giles Constable, "The Historiography of the Crusades," in *The Crusades from the Perspective of Byzantium and the Muslim World*, ed. Angeliki Laiou and Roy Mottahedeh (Washington, DC, 2001), 10–16; Alexander P. Bronisch, *Reconquista und heiliger Krieg: Der Deutung des Krieges im christlichen Spanien von den Westgoten bis ins frühe 12. Jahrhundert* (Münster, 1998), 201–29. Examples of this approach are: Norman Housley, *The Italian Crusades* (Oxford, 1982); Norman Housley, *The Avignon Papacy and the Crusades* (Oxford, 1986); Housley, *The Later Crusades*; Amnon Linder, *Raising Arms: Liturgy in the Struggle to Liberate Jerusalem in the Late Middle Ages* (Turnhout, 2003); Christoph T. Maier, *Preaching the Crusades: Mendicant Friars and the Cross in the Thirteenth Century* (Cambridge, 1994); Christoph T. Maier, *Crusade Propaganda and Ideology* (Cambridge, 2000); Jonathan Riley-Smith, *What Were the Crusades?* (London, 1977, and succeeding editions); Jonathan Riley-Smith, *The Crusades: A History*, 2nd ed. (London, 2005), Jonathan Riley-Smith, ed., *The Atlas of the Crusades* (London, 1991); Jonathan Riley-Smith, ed., *The Oxford Illustrated History of the Crusades* (Oxford, 1995); Elizabeth Siberry, *Criticism of Crusading, 1095–1274* (Oxford, 1985).

2. Examples are Marcus Bull, *Knightly Piety and the Lay Response to the First Crusade: The Limousin and Gascony, c. 970–c. 1130* (Oxford, 1993); Marcus Bull, "Views of Muslims and of Jerusalem in Miracle Stories, c. 1000–c. 1200: Reflections on the Study of First Crusaders' Motivations," in *The Experience of Crusading: Volume One*, ed. Marcus Bull and Norman Housley (Cambridge, 2003); Jonathan Riley-Smith, *The First Crusaders, 1095–1131* (Cambridge, 1997);

Jonathan Riley-Smith, *The Crusades: A History*; James Powell, *Anatomy of a Crusade* (Philadelphia, 1986); Simon Lloyd, *English Society and the Crusade, 1216–1307* (Oxford, 1988); Caroline Smith, *Crusading in the Age of Joinville* (Aldershot, 2006).

3. Peter Watson, *War on the Mind: The Military Uses and Abuses of Psychology* (London, 1978), 246; John Keegan, *The Face of Battle* (London, 1976), 327–29.

4. See William E. Lunt, *Papal Revenues in the Middle Ages* (New York, 1934), 1:71–77; William E. Lunt, *Financial Relations of the Papacy with England* (Cambridge, MA, 1939–62), 1:240–460, 2:75–168; Lloyd, *English Society*, 134–53.

5. Housley, *The Avignon Papacy*, 241–59.

6. Gary Dickson, *The Children's Crusade* (Basingstoke, 2008), 3–6.

7. Eva Haverkamp in the introduction to her edition of *Hebräische Berichte über die Judenverfolgungen während des Ersten Kreuzzugs*, MGH Hebräische Texte aus dem mittelalterlichen Deutschland I (Hanover, 2005), 14–24.

8. For a critical reinterpretation of this view, see Robert Chazan, *Medieval Stereotypes and Modern Antisemitism* (Berkeley, 1997).

9. See Robert Chazan, *European Jewry and the First Crusade* (Berkeley, 1987); Jeremy Cohen, *Sanctifying the Name of God: Jewish Martyrs and Jewish Memories of the First Crusade* (Philadelphia, 2004).

10. Ronnie Ellenblum, *Crusader Castles and Modern Histories* (Cambridge, 2007), 61.

11. Rowan Williams, archbishop of Canterbury, "What is Christianity?" Lecture given at the International Islamic University in Islamabad, Pakistan, November 23, 2005, www.archbishopofcanterbury.org/sermons_speeches/2005/051123.htm.

12. Professor Diarmaid MacCulloch, in publicity material for Christopher Tyerman, *God's War: A New History of the Crusades* (London, 2006).

13. For St. Francis, see Maier, *Preaching the Crusades*, 9–17.

14. Lateran I: 10 (1123), although its status as a general council has been questioned; Lateran IV: 3, 71 (1215); Lyons I: [2, 3] (1245); Lyons II: 1 (1274); Vienne: bulla 1 (1311–12); Lateran V: sessio 9 (1514). *Conciliorum Oecumenicorum Decreta*, ed. Giuseppe Alberigo et al. (Freiburg, 1962).

15. Norman Housley, *Religious Warfare in Europe, 1400–1536* (Oxford, 2002), 87.

16. Paul Rousset, "Un Huguenot propose une croisade: Le projet de François de la Noue (1580–1585)," *Zeitschrift für Schweizerische Kirchengeschichte (Revue d'histoire ecclésiastique suisse)* 72 (1978): 333–44.

17. The author was Ramzi bin al-Shibh. Extracts in translation were published on the Web site of *The Sunday Times* (London) on September 8, 2002.

18. Jonathan Riley-Smith, "Islam and the Crusades in History and Imagination, 8 November 1898–11 September 2001," *Crusades* 2 (2003): 151–67. For other treatments, see Edward Peters, "The *Firanj* are coming—again," *Orbis* 48 (2004): 3–17; Christopher Tyerman, *Fighting for Christendom: Holy War and the Crusades* (Oxford, 2004), 201–10; Housley, *Contesting the Crusades*, 156–66; Riley-Smith, *The Crusades: A History*, 304–7.

19. Kenneth M. Setton, *The Papacy and the Levant (1204–1571)*, 4 vols. (Philadelphia, 1976–84); Kenneth M. Setton, *Venice, Austria, and the Turks in the Seventeenth Century* (Philadelphia, 1991).

20. Elizabeth Siberry, "Images of the Crusades in the Nineteenth and Twentieth Centuries," *The Oxford Illustrated History of the Crusades*, ed. Jonathan Riley-Smith (Oxford, 1995), 364–85; Elizabeth Siberry, *The New Crusaders: Images of the Crusades in the Nineteenth and Early Twentieth Centuries* (Aldershot, 2000).

21. Werner Ende, "Wer ist ein Glaubensheld, wer ist ein Ketzer," *Die Welt des Islams* NS 23 (1984); Carole Hillenbrand, *The Crusades: Islamic Perspectives* (Edinburgh, 1999), 589–616; Emanuel Sivan, "Modern Arab Historiography of the Crusades," *Asian and African Studies* 8 (1972).

1. CRUSADES AS CHRISTIAN HOLY WARS

1. Norman Housley, *Contesting the Crusades* (Oxford, 2006), 1–23.

2. Jonathan Riley-Smith, *What Were the Crusades?*, 3rd ed. (Basingstoke, 2002).

3. Exodus 20–23, 32:15–29.

4. Matthew 8:5–13; Luke 7:1–10. For John the Baptist, see Luke 3:14.

5. Luke 22:36–38.

6. Luke 22:50–51. See also Matthew 26:51–54; Mark 14:47; John 18:10–11.

7. Shortly before the First Crusade this was to be interpreted as justifying the pope's authority over the use of force. John of Mantua, "Tractatus in Cantica Canticorum," in *Ioannis Mantuani in Cantica Canticorum et De Sancta Maria Tractatus ad Comitissam Matildam,* ed. Bernhard Bischoff and Burkhard Taeger (Freiburg, 1973), 52.

8. Romans 13:4.

9. John Helgeland, "The Early Church and War: The Sociology of Idolatry," in *Peace in a Nuclear Age,* ed. Charles J. Reid (Washington, DC, 1986), 34–47.

10. For Augustine's thinking on violence, see Frederick H. Russell, *The*

Just War in the Middle Ages (Cambridge, 1975), 16–26; Jonathan Riley-Smith, "Crusading as an Act of Love," *History* 65 (1980): 185–87.

11. Augustine of Hippo, *De civitate Dei*, xix, 7, ed. Bernard Dombart and Alphonse Kalb (*CCSL* 47–8, Turnhout, 1955), 48:672.

12. Augustine of Hippo, *Quaestionum in Heptateuchum Libri VII*, vi, 10, ed. Benedikt Schwank (*CCSL* 33, Turnhout, 1958), 319.

13. Augustine of Hippo, "Contra Faustum Manichaeum", xxii, 75–9, *PL* 42:448–51.

14. Augustine of Hippo, *De civitate Dei* i, 27, *CCSL* 47:26–27; Augustine of Hippo, *Quaestionum in Heptateuchum* vi, 10, *CCSL* 33:319.

15. Riley-Smith, "Crusading as an Act of Love," 185.

16. See Jean Flori, *L'Essor de Chevalerie XIe–XIIe siècles* (Geneva, 1986), 182–84; Riley-Smith, *The First Crusaders*, 47–48.

17. Augustine of Hippo, "Contra Faustum Manichaeum," xxii, 74, *PL* 42:447.

18. Riley-Smith, "Crusading as an Act of Love," 186–87.

19. Russell, *The Just War*, 300–4. See also H. E. John Cowdrey, "Christianity and the Morality of Warfare During the First Century of Crusading," in *The Experience of Crusading, Volume One: Western Approaches*, ed. Marcus Bull and Norman Housley (Cambridge, 2003), 186–91.

20. Alberico Gentili and Hugo Grotius played major roles in the process. Heinz Duchhardt, "La guerre et le droit des gens dans l'Europe du XVIe au XVIIIe siècle," in *Guerre et concurrence entre les Etats européens du XIVe au XVIIIe siècle*, ed. Philippe Contamine (Paris, 1998), 344–56.

21. Denis Diderot and Jean Le Rond d'Alembert, *Encyclopédie* (Paris, 1751–65), 4:505.

22. Duchhardt, "La guerre," 358–64.

23. See Cowdrey, "Christianity," 175. A summary of modern opinions on the history of Christian holy war can be found in Alexander P. Bronisch, *Reconquista und heiliger Krieg: Die Deutung des Krieges im christlichen Spanien von den Westgoten bis ins frühe 12. Jahrhundert* (Münster, 1998), 201–29.

24. James of Vitry, "Sermo ad fratres ordinis militaris," in *Analecta novissima,* ed. Jean Baptiste Pitra (Paris, 1888), 2:419.

25. Iben Fonnesberg-Schmidt, *The Popes and the Baltic Crusades, 1147–1254* (Leiden, 2007), 32–33, 91–94; Benjamin Z. Kedar, *Crusade and Mission: European Approaches Toward the Muslims* (Princeton, 1984).

26. Riley-Smith, *What Were the Crusades?*, 18–20.

27. James Brundage, *Medieval Canon Law and the Crusader* (Madison, 1969), 30–115.

28. Humbert of Romans, "Opus tripartitum," in *Fasciculus rerum expeten-darum et fugiendarum*, ed. Edward Brown (London, 1690), 2:191–98.

29. See Elizabeth Siberry, *Criticism of Crusading, 1095–1274* (Oxford, 1985), 156–89.

30. Lamentations 5:2.; John of Abbeville, "Sermo ad crucesignatos," *The Preaching of the Crusades to the Holy Land, 1095–1270*, ed. Penny J. Cole (Cambridge, MA, 1991), 222.

31. This topic will be discussed in a forthcoming publication by Dr. William Purkis.

32. Norman Housley, *The Later Crusades, 1274–1580* (Oxford, 1992), 337–39.

33. Norman Housley, *The Italian Crusades* (Oxford, 1982), 35–62.

34. Peter the Venerable, *The Letters*, ed. Giles Constable, (Cambridge, MA, 1967), 1:409.

35. James Muldoon, *Popes, Lawyers, and Infidels* (Liverpool, 1979), 6–7.

36. For the history of the title of vicar of Christ, see Michele Maccarone, *Vicarius Christi: Storia del titole papale* (Rome, 1952), 11–154.

37. *Actes des comtes de Flandre 1071–1128*, ed. Fernand Vercauteren (Brussels, 1938), 63.

38. *Die Kreuzzugsbriefe aus den Jahren 1088–1100*, ed. Heinrich Hagenmeyer (Innsbruck, 1901), 164.

39. Jonathan Riley-Smith, *The First Crusade and the Idea of Crusading* (London, 1986), 91–92; Riley-Smith, *The First Crusaders*, 77–78.

40. Robert of Rheims, "Historia Iherosolimitana," *RHC Oc* 3:723. See Riley-Smith, *The First Crusade*, 135–52.

41. Baldric of Bourgueil, "Historia Jerosolimitana," *RHC Oc* 4:15.

42. Gunther of Pairis, *Hystoria Constantinopolitana*, ed. Peter Orth (Spolia Berolinensia 5, Hildesheim and Zürich, 1994), 113.

43. Innocent III, "Quia maior," in *Studien zum Register Innocenz III*, ed. Georgine Tangl (Weimar, 1929), 88–89.

44. Baldric of Bourgueil, 101.

45. See for example Innocent III, "Quia maior," 89–90.

46. James of Vitry, "Sermo I ad crucesignatos vel–signandos" in *Crusade Propaganda*, ed. Maier, 98.

47. James of Vitry, "Sermo ad fratres ordinis militaris," 419.

48. John of Joinville, *Vie de Saint Louis*, ed. Jacques Montfrin (Paris, 1995), 240.

49. Innocent III, "Experimento didicimus," *PL* 215:1339.

50. Denys Pringle, *The Churches of the Crusader Kingdom of Jerusalem: A Corpus*

(Cambridge, 1993–), 3:68; Jaroslav Folda, *Crusader Art in the Holy Land from the Third Crusade to the Fall of Acre, 1187–1291* (Cambridge, 2005), 162–63.

51. Matthew Paris, *Chronica maiora*, ed. Henry R. Luard (London 1872–83, Rolls Series 57), 3:373. See Lloyd, *English Society and the Crusade*, 82–83, 100, 176, 179, 193–94, app. 3 (1); Christopher Tyerman, *England and the Crusades* (Chicago and London, 1988), 97–99.

52. But compare Maurice Keen, *Chivalry* (New Haven and London, 1984), 16–17.

53. Riley-Smith, "Crusading as an Act of Love," 185.

54. *Papsturkunden für Templer und Johanniter*, ed. Rudolf Hiestand (Vorarbeiten zum Oriens Pontificius I-II), 2 vols. (Göttingen, 1972–84), 2:96.

55. Jonathan Riley-Smith, *The Knights of St. John in Jerusalem and Cyprus c. 1050–1310* (London, 1967), 41–52. See "A Twelfth-Century Description of the Jerusalem Hospital," ed. Benjamin Z. Kedar, in *The Military Orders: Volume 2*, ed. Helen Nicholson (Aldershot, 1998), 3–26; "Administrative Regulations for the Hospital of St. John in Jerusalem dating from the 1180s," ed. Susan Edgington, *Crusades* 4 (2005), 21–37.

56. Riley-Smith, *The First Crusaders*, 163–64.

57. *Papsturkunden für Templer und Johanniter*, 2:222–30.

58. Alexander III, "Piam admodum," in *Cartulaire général de l'ordre des Hospitaliers de St Jean de Jérusalem*, ed. Joseph Delaville Le Roulx, (Paris, 1894–1906), 1:360–61.

59. Alexander III, "Quam amabilis Deo," *Papsturkunden für Templer und Johanniter* 2:159–62; and see Hiestand's commentary on 136–62, esp. 150–51.

60. *Cartulaire général de l'ordre des Hospitaliers*, 1:426.

61. Ibid., 1:429.

62. "A Twelfth-Century Description," 21–22.

63. Bernard of Clairvaux, "Epistolae," in *Sancti Bernardi Opera*, ed. Jean Leclercq et al. (Rome, 1957–77), 8:314.

64. Gregory VIII, "Audita tremendi," in "Historia de expeditione Friderici imperatoris," ed. Anton Chroust, *MGH Scriptores rerum Germanicarum*, n.s. 5 (Berlin, 1928), 9.

65. Innocent III, "Protector in se," *PL* 216:704.

66. Gianpietro Contarini, *Historia delle cose successe dal principio della guerra mossa da Selim Ottomano a' Venetiani* (Venice, 1572), fol. 49v. Cited by Norman Housley, *Documents on the Later Crusades, 1274–1580* (Basingstoke, 1996), 192.

67. Bernard of Clairvaux, "De consideratione,"in *Sancti Bernardi Opera* 3:410–11. For the *"peccatis exigentibus hominum"* theme, see Siberry, *Criticism of Crusading*, 69–89.

68. See Siberry, *Criticism of Crusading*, 98–108.

69. Gregory VIII, "Audita tremendi," 8–9.

70. See Jonathan Riley-Smith, "Christian Violence and the Crusades," in *Religious Violence Between Christians and Jews*, ed. Anna Sapir Abulafia (Basingstoke, 2002), 9–10.

71. Emmanuel Sivan, *L'Islam et la croisade* (Paris, 1968), 70–72.

72. Peter Carey, "The Origins of the Java War (1825–30)," *English Historical Review* 91 (1976): 75–78.

73. Hue-Tam Ho Tai, *Millenarianism and Peasant Politics in Vietnam* (Cambridge, MA, 1983).

74. Michael Adas, *Prophets of Rebellion* (Cambridge, 1979).

75. Innocent III, "Licet circa statutum," in *Innocent III, Die Register*, ed. Othmar Hageneder et al. (Graz, Cologne, Rome, and Vienna, 1964–), 1:809.

76. Peter of Vaux-de-Cernay, *Hystoria Albigensis*, ed. Pascal Guébin and Ernest Lyon (Paris, 1926), 1:64–65.

77. See, for example, *Vetera monumenta historica Hungariam sacram illustrantia*, ed. Augustin Theiner (Rome, 1859–60), 1:178–79.

78. See Chazan, *European Jewry and the First Crusade*; Cohen, *Sanctifying the Name of God*.

79. For example Bernard of Clairvaux, "Epistolae," 8:316–17; Peter the Venerable, *The Letters* 1:328; *The Apostolic See and the Jews: Documents*, ed. Shlomo Simonsohn, (Toronto, 1988–91), 1:86–7, 92–3.

80. Ekkehard of Aura, "Hierosolymita," *RHC Oc* 5:20. See Richard of Poitiers, "Chronicon," *RHGF* 12:411–12; Guibert of Nogent, *De vita sua*, ed. Edmond René Labande (Paris, 1981), 246–48.

2. CRUSADES AS CHRISTIAN PENITENTIAL WARS

1. Guibert of Nogent, *Dei gesta per Francos*, ed. Robert B. C. Huygens (CCCM 127A, Turnholt, 1996), 198–99. See also Orderic Vitalis, *Historia aecclesiastica*, ed. and trans. Marjorie Chibnall (Oxford, 1969–79), 5:28.

2. *De expugnatione Lyxbonensi*, ed. Charles W. David (New York, 1936), 56.

3. Norman Housley, *The Italian Crusades* (Oxford, 1982), 40–70, 164.

4. See Christoph T. Maier, "Crisis, Liturgy, and the Crusade in the Twelfth and Thirteenth Centuries," *Journal of Ecclesiastical History* 48 (1997): 638–57.

5. Henry of Livonia, *Chronicon Livoniae*, ed. Leonid Arbusow and Adolf Bauer, (*MGH Scriptores rerum Germanicarum*, n.s. 31, 2nd ed., Hanover, 1955), 132.

6. Nurith Kenaan-Kedar and Benjamin Kedar, "The Significance of a Twelfth-Century Sculptural Group: *Le Retour du Croisé*," in *Dei gesta per Francos*,

ed. Michel Balard, Benjamin Z. Kedar, and Jonathan Riley-Smith (Aldershot, 2001), 29–44.

7. Albert of Aachen, *Historia Ierosolimitana*, ed. Susan Edgington (Oxford, 2007), 474.

8. *Saint-Denis de Nogent-le-Rotrou, 1031–1789, Histoire et cartulaire*, ed. Hector J. H. J. G. de Souancé and Charles Metais (Vannes, 1899), 36–39. The last wish of another knight was that the palms he had collected at Jericho should be laid on the altar of the abbey church of Bèze, of which he was a *confrater*. "Liber memorabilium rerum seu etiam cartarum abbatiae Besensis," in *Spicilegium sive collectio veterum aliquot scriptorum*, ed. Luc d'Achéry (Paris, 1655–77), 1:574.

9. H. E. John Cowdrey, "Christianity and the Morality of Warfare During the First Century of Crusading," in *The Experience of Crusading, Volume One: Western Approaches*, ed. Marcus Bull and Norman Housley (Cambridge, 2003), 181–86. To Augustine of Hippo, who had had little sense of merit, soldiers engaged in a holy war incurred neither credit nor blame, since they were only doing their duty. Jonathan Riley-Smith, "Crusading as an Act of Love," *History* 65 (1980): 187.

10. The significance of the prospect of martyrdom to crusaders has been a subject of debate. See Norman Housley, *Contesting the Crusades* (Oxford, 2006), 41.

11. John of Joinville, *Vie de Saint Louis*, ed. Jacques Montfrin (Paris, 1995), 146. He referred to the subject of martyrdom at least three times in the course of his description of the crusade in which he had been engaged. John of Joinville, 290, 376, 332.

12. Louis IX of France, "Epistola," in *Historiae Francorum Scriptores*, ed. François Du Chesne (Paris, 1636–49), 5:429; Charles of Anjou, "Déposition," in *Notices et documents publiés pour la société de l'histoire de France à l'occasion du cinquantième anniversaire de sa fondation*, ed. Paul E. D. Riant (Paris, 1884), 175.

13. Eudes of Châteauroux, "Sermones in anniversario Roberti comitis Attrabatensis," in *The Preaching of the Crusades to the Holy Land*, ed. Cole, 235–43.

14. The uncertainties led to a ruling by Thomas Aquinas on the question whether those who died before fulfilling their crusade vows could benefit from them. Thomas Aquinas, *Quaestiones Quodlibetales*, ed. Raimundo Spiazzi (Turin, 1956), 36–38, 106.

15. Riley-Smith, *The First Crusaders*, 48–52.

16. Wenrich of Trier, "Epistola sub Theoderici episcopi Virdunensis nomine composite," *MGH Libelli de Lite Imperatorum et Pontificum*, 1:296; Sigebert of Gembloux, "Leodicensium epistola adversus Paschalem Papam," *MGH Libelli de Lite Imperatorum et Pontificum*, 2:464.

17. Gilbert of Tournai, "Sermo III ad crucesignatos et crucesignandos," in *Crusade Propaganda*, ed. Maier, 204.

18. Riley-Smith, *The First Crusaders*, 67.

19. The arguments of Paul Chevedden ["Canon 2 of the Council of Clermont (1095) and the Crusade Indulgence," *Annuarium Historiae Conciliorum* 37 (2005): 253–322] seem to be based on a fundamental misunderstanding of the nature of indulgences.

20. Guibert of Nogent, *Dei gesta*, 87.

21. Jonathan Riley-Smith, *The First Crusade and the Idea of Crusading* (London, 1986), 91–119. Although it is clear that to most of them the crusade had been a one-off experience, never to be repeated. Riley-Smith, *The First Crusaders*, 165–68.

22. Riley-Smith, *The First Crusade and the Idea of Crusading*, 135–52.

23. Baldric of Bourgueil, "Historia Jerosolimitana," *RHC Oc* 4, 101.

24. Ibid., 28.

25. Guibert of Nogent, *Dei gesta*, 233.

26. Riley-Smith, *The First Crusaders*, 70.

27. Humbert of Romans, *De predicatione sancte crucis* (Nuremburg, 1490), chap. xliv.

28. Riley-Smith, *What Were the Crusades?*, 59–64.

29. Humbert of Romans, *De predicatione*, chap. iii.

30. Eudes of Deuil, *De Profectione Ludovici VII in Orientem*, ed. Virginia Berry (New York, 1948), 16.

31. Pope Gregory VIII, "Audita tremendi," in "Historia de expeditione Friderici imperatoris," ed. Anton Chroust, *MGH Scriptores rerum Germanicarum*, n.s. 5 (Berlin, 1928), 9.

32. William C. Jordan, *Louis IX and the Challenge of the Crusade* (Princeton, 1979), 51–63.

33. John of Joinville, 212–14.

34. Jean Richard, *Saint Louis* (Paris, 1983), 570.

35. Riley-Smith, *The First Crusade and the Idea of Crusading*, 82–85.

36. James of Vitry, *Lettres*, ed. Robert B. C. Huygens (Leiden, 1960), 117.

37. John of Joinville, 220.

38. Gianpietro Contarini, fol. 49v.

39. Pope Innocent III, "Quia maior," in *Studien zum Register Innocenz III*, ed. Georgine Tangl (Weimar, 1929), 95–96.

40. Amnon Linder, *Raising Arms: Liturgy in the Struggle to Liberate Jerusalem in the Late Middle Ages* (Turnhout, 2003).

41. Thomas Aquinas, *Summa Theologica* 2a2ae, qu. 188, art. 3.

42. See Giles Constable, "The Place of the Crusader in Medieval Society," *Viator* 29 (1998): 390–403.

43. See, for example, Anthony Luttrell, "The Spiritual Life of the Hospitallers of Rhodes," in *Die Spiritualität der Ritterorden im Mittelater*, ed. Zeon Hubert Nowak (Toruń, 1993), 75–96 [reprinted in Anthony T. Luttrell, *The Hospitaller State on Rhodes and Its Western Provinces, 1306–1462* (Aldershot, 1999), article no. IX]; Tom Licence, "The Templars and the Hospitallers, Christ and the Saints," *Crusades* 4 (2005): 39–57; Tom Licence, "The Military Orders as Monastic Orders," *Crusades* 5 (2006): 39–53. Austerity was visually expressed in the unshaven faces of the Templars and it is striking how often in the accounts of the early fourteenth-century interrogations there are references to brother knights and sergeants who had shaved off their beards to mark their abandonment of their order in the wake of the scandal that was now enveloping it. *Le procès des Templiers*, ed. Jules Michelet, 2 vols. (Paris, 1841–51).

44. Maurice Keen, *Chivalry* (New Haven and London, 1984), 172–74; Werner Paravicini, *Die Preussenreise des Europäsichen Adels* (Sigmaringen, 1989–95), 1:288–344.

45. Jonathan Riley-Smith, *The Knights of St. John in Jerusalem and Cyprus, c. 1050–1310* (London, 1967), 272–73.

46. Sabba di Castiglione, *Ricordi a Fra Bartholomeo di Castiglione suo nipote* (Bologna, 1549).

47. Innocent III, "Gaudemus in Domino," *PL* 216:907; Riley-Smith, *The First Crusaders*, 54–60.

48. See Jonathan Phillips, "St. Bernard of Clairvaux, The Low Countries, and the Lisbon Letter of the Second Crusade," *Journal of Ecclesiastical History* 48 (1997): 487–89.

49. Gerald of Wales, "Itinerarium Cambriae," in *Opera*, ed. James Francis Dimock (Rolls Series 21/6, London, 1868), 13–147.

50. "Historia de expeditione Friderici imperatoris," ed. Anton Chroust, *Monumenta Germaniae historica. Scriptores rerum Germanicarum*, n.s. 5 (Berlin, 1928), 10–15.

51. Innocent III, "Gaudemus in Domino", col. 907. See Riley-Smith, *What Were the Crusades?*, 39–41.

52. Oliver of Paderborn, *Schriften*, ed. Hermann Hoogeweg (Tübingen, 1894), 285–86.

53. Michele Maccarone, "Orvieto e la predicazione della crociata," *Studi su Innocenzo III* (*Italia sacra* 17, Padua, 1972), 161–63.

54. Alfons Becker, *Papst Urban II* (*1088–1099*) (Stuttgart, 1964–88), 2:435–57.

55. "Historia de expeditione Friderici imperatoris," 14–15.

56. Simon Lloyd, *English Society and the Crusade, 1216–1307* (Oxford, 1988), 55–56.

57. Riley-Smith, *The First Crusaders*, 58.

58. Eudes of Deuil, 8.

59. Maccarone, "Orvieto," 132–34.

60. Helmold of Bosau, "Chronica Slavorum," *MGHS* 21:33–4; "Annalista Saxo," *MGHS* 6:728.

61. Matthew Paris, *Chronica maiora* 5:246–47.

62. Eudes of Deuil, 8.

63. Ibn Shaddad, *The Rare and Excellent History of Saladin*, trans. Donald Sidney Richards (Aldershot, 2001), 125.

64. Oliver of Paderborn, 285.

65. Gregory VIII, "Audita tremendi," 6.

66. Humbert of Romans, *De predicatione*, chap. ii.

67. Ibid., chap. i.

68. Landulf the Younger, "Historia Mediolanensis," *MGHS* 20:22.

69. Riley-Smith, *The First Crusaders*, 11.

70. Eudes of Deuil, 8.

71. "Bessarions Instruktion für die Kreuzzugspredigt in Venedig (1463)," ed. Ludwig Mohler, *Römische Quartalschrift* 35 (1927): 342.

72. Maier, *Crusade Propaganda*, 3–68.

73. Seventeen related to crusading to the East, seven to crusades against heretics, and three to a crusade against a Muslim settlement in southern Italy. They are edited in Penny J. Cole, *The Preaching of the Crusades to the Holy Land, 1095–1270* (Cambridge, MA, 1991), 222–43; Maier, *Crusade Propaganda*, 82–229; Christoph T. Maier, "Crusade and Rhetoric Against the Muslim Colony of Lucera: Eudes of Châteauroux's *Sermones de Rebellione Sarracenorum Lucherie in Apulia*," *Journal of Medieval History* 21 (1995): 376–85. I have also read five unpublished sermons for the Albigensian Crusade in transcripts kindly provided by Dr. Christoph Maier.

74. Humbert of Romans, "Opus tripartitum"; Humbert of Romans, *De predicatione*.

75. Rowan Williams, "What is Christianity?" Lecture given at the International Islamic University in Islamabad, Pakistan, November 23, 2005, www.archbishopofcanterbury.org/sermons_speeches/2005/051123.htm.

76. Humbert of Romans, "Sermo I ad peregrinos crucesignatos," in *Crusade Propaganda*, ed. Maier, 212.

77. Eudes of Châteauroux, "Sermo V ad invitandam ad crucem," in *Crusade Propaganda*, ed. Maier, 170.

78. James of Vitry, "Sermo II ad crucesignatos vel–signandos," in *Crusade Propaganda*, ed. Maier, 112. See also Roger of Salisbury, "Sermo ad crucesignatos," in *The Preaching of the Crusades*, ed. Cole, 230; Gilbert of Tournai, "Sermo III," 202; Eudes of Châteauroux, "Sermo I ad assumendam crucem," in *Crusade Propaganda*, ed. Maier, 138; Eudes of Châteauroux, "Sermo IV de invitatione ad crucem," in *Crusade Propaganda*, ed. Maier, 164.

79. Eudes of Châteauroux, "Sermo III de invitatione ad crucem," in *Crusade Propaganda*, ed. Maier, 156.

80. Eudes of Châteauroux, "Sermo I," 130–32. See also Gilbert of Tournai, "Sermo I ad crucesignatos et crucesignandos," in *Crusade Propaganda*, ed. Maier, 184.

81. Humbert of Romans, *De predicatione*, chap. xix.

82. Riley-Smith, *The First Crusaders*, 62–63.

83. Eudes of Châteauroux, "Sermo II de invitatio ad crucem," in *Crusade Propaganda*, ed. Maier, 146

84. Humbert of Romans, *De predicatione*, chap. v. See Cole, *The Preaching of the Crusades*, 206.

85. Roger of Salisbury, "Sermo," 230.

86. James of Vitry, "Sermo II," 108.

87. Humbert of Romans, *De predicatione*, chap. vii. See also Roger of Salisbury, "Sermo," 227–28; James of Vitry, "Sermo I," 86; James of Vitry, "Sermo II," 106–8; Eudes of Châteauroux, "Sermo IV," 160–62; Gilbert of Tournai, "Sermo I," 180–88; Gilbert of Tournai, "Sermo III," 208.

88. "The Elstow Sermon," in *The Preaching of the Crusades*, ed. Cole, 232–34; and see also 173–76.

89. Ronnie Ellenblum, *Frankish Rural Settlement in the Latin Kingdom of Jerusalem* (Cambridge, 1998).

90. Freddy Thiriet, *La Romanie Vénitienne au Moyen Age* (Paris, 1959); Philip Argenti, *The Occupation of Chios by the Genoese and their Administration of the Island, 1346–1566*, 3 vols. (Cambridge, 1958).

91. Norman Housley, *The Later Crusades, 1274–1580* (Oxford, 1992), 322–75.

92. See Luis Adão Fonseca, "As Ordens Militares e a Expansão," *A Alta Nobreza e a Fundação do Estado da Índia* (Lisbon, 2004), 325–47. Luis Adão Fonseca, "La storiografia dell'espansione marittima portoghese (secc. XIV–XV)," *Bullettino dell'Istituto Storico Italiano per il Medio Evo* 106 (2004), 299–346; Isabel Morgado S. E. Silva and Maria Cristina Pimenta, "As Ordens de Santiago e de Cristo e a Fundação do Estado da Índia. Uma Perspectiva de Estudo," *A Alta Nobreza e a Fundação do Estado da Índia* (Lisbon, 2004), 349–87.

93. See Michael M. Postan, "The Trade of Medieval Europe: The North,"

in *The Cambridge Economic History of Europe*, vol. 2, 2nd ed. (Cambridge, 1987), 212.

94. Jonathan Riley-Smith, "Casualties and the Number of Knights on the First Crusade," *Crusades* 1 (2002): 13–28; Powell, *Anatomy of a Crusade*, 166–72.

95. Riley-Smith, *The First Crusaders*, 113–35.

96. Francisco Augusto Garcez Teixeira, *Tomar* (Porto, 1929), 5–11.

97. Hannibal P. Scicluna, *The Church of St. John in Valletta* (San Martin, 1955); Nicholas de Piro, *The Temple of the Knights of Malta* (Sliema, 1999); Dane Munro, *Memento Mori*, 2 vols. (Valletta, 2005).

3. CRUSADING AND IMPERIALISM

1. Cardinal Simeoni was not keen. François Renault, *Lavigerie, l'Esclavage Africain et l'Europe, 1868–92* (Paris 1971), 1:253.

2. For his life, see François Renault, *Cardinal Lavigerie: Churchman, Prophet, and Missionary*, trans. John O'Donohue (London, 1994).

3. In October 1880 a motley group of mercenaries—two Frenchmen, two Belgians, and four Dutchmen—was subjected to a ceremony in the cathedral of Algiers, during which, following what he thought was an ancient rite of knighthood, Lavigerie blessed their arms before they set out with a caravan of missionaries for Lake Tanganyika. Renault, *Lavigerie*, 1:247.

4. Renault, *Lavigerie*, 1:252–53.

5. Ibid., 1:253.

6. Ibid., 1:253–55.

7. Bernd Schwenk, *Calatrava: Entstehung und Frühgeschichte eines Spanischen Ritterordens Zisterziensischer Observanz im 12. Jahrhundert* (Münster, 1992), 49–103.

8. Renault, *Lavigerie*, 1:255.

9. Leo XIII, "Solemne semper," ed. Michel de Pierredon, *Histoire Politique de l'Ordre Souverain de Saint-Jean de Jérusalem (Ordre de Malte) de 1789 à 1955*, 2nd ed. (Paris, 1990–), 3:260.

10. Renault, *Lavigerie*, 1:255–60.

11. Ibid., 1:260–1.

12. Ibid., 2:74–5.

13. Ibid., 2:82–5.

14. Leo XIII, "Inclytam antiquitate originis," in *Histoire Politique*, ed. Pierredon, 3:269.

15. Renault, *Lavigerie*, 2:85.

16. Ibid., 2:85–86.

17. Ibid., 2:87–93.

18. Ibid., 2:97–105.

19. Ibid., 2:389–91.

20. Archivio Generale dei Missionari d'Africa (A.G.M.Afr.) Ms. B.16.82. I am very grateful to the archivist of the White Fathers for providing me with a photocopy of this manuscript. There is a summary of it in Renault, *Lavigerie*, 2:392–3.

21. Renault, *Lavigerie*, 2:394–407. One brother, Joseph Lachelin, who had already withdrawn from the institute the previous September, composed a rule for an *Ordre des Pionniers Africains du Sacré-Coeur de Jésus* and submitted it to the missionary fathers of the Saint-Esprit, asking for help to go to Chad. He was enthusiastically supported by Father Yung, a White Father novice who had been at Biskra at the time of the dissolution and had protested vehemently against it. Yung joined Lachelin and at the beginning of 1894 they founded a *Société Française des Pionniers Africains* to extend French power in Africa and abolish slavery. They published a monthly bulletin with the title of *La France Noire*. They announced the departure of four pioneers to Madagascar and tried to get support for their rule from the papacy. Yung's crazy plans and hyperbolic language were thought to be compromising missions and the White Fathers put a stop to his campaign. Renault, *Lavigerie*, 2:407–9.

22. Michel de Pierredon, *Histoire Politique de l'Ordre Souverain de Saint-Jean de Jérusalem (Ordre de Malte) de 1789 à 1955*, 2nd ed. (Paris, 1990–2000), 3:1–68; Henry J.A. Sire, *The Knights of Malta* (New Haven and London, 1994), 251–53; Maximilian von Twickel, "Die nationalen Assoziationen des Malteserordens in Deutschland," *Der Johanniterorden, Der Malteserorden*, ed. Adam Wienand (Cologne, 1970), 471–78.

23. Renault, *Cardinal Lavigerie*, 377.

24. Ibid., 427.

25. See Fonnesberg-Schmidt, *The Popes and the Baltic Crusades*.

26. For events in Africa, see Thomas Pakenham, *The Scramble for Africa* (London, 1991).

27. They recognized, for example, the movement's historical significance and its achievements. Ronnie Ellenblum, *Crusader Castles and Modern Histories* (Cambridge, 2007), 3–12.

28. Napoleon I, *Mémoires et Oeuvres*, ed. Tancrède Martel (Paris, 1910), 246.

29. Harold M. Acton, *The Bourbons of Naples (1734–1825)* (London, 1956; repr. 1974), 340–44.

30. Ellenblum, *Crusader Castles*, 10–17.

31. Joseph-François Michaud, *Histoire des croisades*, 4th ed. (Paris, 1825–29), 1:510–11.

32. Ibid., 1:524.

33. Claire Constans and Philippe Lamarque, *Les Salles des Croisades: Château de Versailles* (Versailles, 2002); Elizabeth Siberry, *The New Crusaders: Images of the Crusades in the Nineteenth and Early Twentieth Centuries* (Aldershot, 2000), 51–53, 169–70, 208–11; Ellenblum, *Crusader Castles*, 18–23; David Abulafia, "Invented Italians in the Courtois Charters," in *Crusade and Settlement*, ed. Peter W. Edbury (Cardiff, 1985), 135–43.

34. Siberry, *The New Crusaders*, 53; Ellenblum, *Crusader Castles*, 26–27.

35. Siberry, *The New Crusaders*, 53–54.

36. Siberry, *The New Crusaders*, 169; Ellenblum, *Crusader Castles*, 23–26.

37. Adam Knobler, "Saint Louis and French Political Culture," in *Medievalism in Europe II: Studies in Medievalism*, ed. Leslie J. Workman and Kathleen Verduin, (Cambridge, 1996), 164.

38. Norman Daniel, *Islam, Europe, and Empire* (Edinburgh, 1966), 345.

39. For what follows, see Jonathan Riley-Smith, "The Order of St. John in England, 1827–1858," in *The Military Orders: Fighting for the Faith and Caring for the Sick*, ed. Malcolm Barber (Aldershot, 1994), 121–38.

40. See Pierredon, *Histoire Politique* 2:137–60, esp. 137–48.

41. MVO, Historical Memoranda, 1:98.

42. MVO, Richard Woof, *Order of St John of Jerusalem in England* (1872), proof, opp. 13; MVO, Historical Memoranda, 1:238–39, 243; 3:133; MVO, OSJ Anglia Minutes, 107; Pierredon, *Histoire Politique* 2:198–298.

43. See Matthew Smith Anderson, *The Eastern Question, 1774–1923* (London, 1966), 53–58.

44. Pierredon, *Histoire Politique* 2:211–15; and see 205–59, 269. See also MVO, Historical Memoranda, 1:105, 242–43; MVO, Woof, 6–7; Edouard Driault and Michel Lhéritier, *Histoire diplomatique de la Grèce de 1821 à nos jours*, 5 vols. (Paris, 1925–26), 1:208–15.

45. MVO, Ms K 8/1 (bonds); Pierredon, *Histoire Politique*, 2:245–46 (extracts from printed prospectus); MVO, Historical Memoranda, 1:7 (copy of the prospectus), 121 (transcripts of press comment).

46. MVO, Historical Memoranda, 1:85–86; MVO, OSJ Anglia Minutes, 24, 26; BASMOM, Letter Book 1:30; Pierredon, *Histoire Politique*, 2:257–58, 260–72, 289.

47. MVO, First Instrument of Convention, Ms K 32/4. (Translation in MVO, Historical Memoranda, 1:43–49).

48. MVO, Archives § 57; MVO, Copies of Documents, 96; MVO, Rob-

ert Bigsby, notes in OSJ Anglia Minutes, 386–87; MVO, Historical Memoranda, 1:244–45 (visiting card); also 75, 101–3, 105, 243–48; 3:226.

49. MVO, Bigsby, notes in OSJ Anglia Minutes, 377, 384; MVO, Historical Memoranda, 1:243, 247; 3:133.

50. MVO, First, Second, and Third Instruments of Convention, Mss K 32/4; MVO, Historical Memoranda 1:43–49; MVO, OSJ Anglia Minutes 3, 5–11. See also Pierredon, *Histoire Politique*, 2:291–93.

51. MVO, Letter of Instruction, Ms K 32/4; MVO, Copies of Documents, 1–9, 82–83; MVO, OSJ Anglia Minutes, 6–7; MVO, Bigsby, notes in OSJ Anglia Minutes, 389. See also MVO, Copies of Documents, 74–75.

52. Udo Arnold, "Eight Hundred Years of the Teutonic Order," *The Military Orders: Fighting for the Faith and Caring for the Sick*, ed. Malcolm Barber (Aldershot, 1994), 231–32.

53. Sire, *The Knights of Malta*, 225.

54. MVO, Copies of Documents, 60–71, 72–82; MVO, OSJ Anglia Minutes, 11–12; MVO, Bigsby, notes in OSJ Anglia Minutes, 383. See also Pierredon, *Histoire Politique*, 2:295–96. See as an example of recruitment MVO, Historical Memoranda, 1:123.

55. Siberry, *The New Crusaders*, 76–82; and see 203–7 for Sir William's pamphlet.

56. MVO, OSJ Anglia Minutes, 30–39.

57. BASMOM, Letter Book, 1:54–55; MVO, OSJ Anglia Minutes, 354.

58. In *Sybil*. See *Oxford Dictionary of National Biography*, ed. Henry C. G. Matthews and Brian Harrison (Oxford, 2004), 7:997–98. "He compiled a book, *Broun's Baronetage*, in which he filled the preface with twenty pages of his own arguments and gave his own family three times as much space as anybody else's." Ian Anstruther, *The Knight and the Umbrella* (London, 1963), 80–81.

59. BASMOM, Letter Book, 1:18–20, 24; see also 38.

60. For the ambulance movement, see Ronnie Cole-Mackintosh, *A Century of Service to Mankind* (London, 1986), 81–87.

61. See Kim Munholland, "Michaud's *History of the Crusades* and the French Crusade in Algeria under Louis Philippe," *The Popularization of Images*, ed. Petra ten-Doesschate Chu and Gabriel P. Weisberg (Princeton, 1994), 154; Knobler, "Saint Louis," 159–61.

62. Munholland, "Michaud's *History*," 163–64; Siberry, *The New Crusaders*, 82.

63. Knobler, "Saint Louis," 163–64.

64. Knobler, "Saint Louis," 164.

65. Claude R. Conder, *The Latin Kingdom of Jerusalem, 1099 to 1291 AD* (London, 1897), 428; Siberry, *The New Crusaders*, 26.

66. Siberry, *The New Crusaders*, 26; Ellenblum, *Crusader Castles*, 47–48.

67. Hillenbrand, *The Crusades*, 604; Siberry, *The New Crusaders*, 95–96.

68. Knobler, 168.

69. Sivan, "Modern Arab Historiography," 117; Ellenblum, *Crusader Castles*, 46–47. For examples, see Jean Longnon, *Les français d'Outremer au moyen-âge* (Paris, 1929), 333–34; René Grousset, *Histoire des croisades* (Paris, 1934–36), 3:763.

70. For example, see James W. Thompson, *An Economic and Social History of the Middle Ages (300–1300)* (New York, 1928), 380–435. See also *The Cambridge Economic History of Europe*, (Cambridge, 1941–89), 1:69.

71. To Geoffrey Barraclough in 1970, claiming (falsely) to speak for all historians, "our verdict" was that the Latin settlements in the east were "radically unstable centers of colonial exploitation." Cited in Constable, "The Historiography of the Crusades," 3. Marxists have, rather oddly, never had much to say about the Crusades. See Bull, "Views of Muslims and of Jerusalem," 18; Housley, *Contesting the Crusades*, 77–78.

4. CRUSADING AND ISLAM

1. *The Times* (London), November 1, 1898, November 16, 1898; Georges Gaulis, *La ruine d'une empire: Abd-ul-Hamid, ses amis et ses peuples* (Paris, 1913), 124, 163–79 (who commented that in the circumstances the kaiser's dress struck him as being "a little too theatrical"); Elizabeth Siberry, *The New Crusaders: Images of the Crusades in the Nineteenth and Early Twentieth Centuries* (Aldershot, 2000), 67; William Treloar, *With the Kaiser in the East, 1898* (London, 1915), 22. See also Giles MacDonogh, *The Last Kaiser: William the Impetuous* (London, 2000), 237; Alan Palmer, *The Kaiser: Warlord of the Second Reich* (London, 1978), 91–92.

2. *The Times*, November 10, 1898; Werner Ende, "Wer ist ein Glaubensheld, wer ist ein Ketzer," *Die Welt des Islams* NS 23 (1984), 79–84; Gaulis, *La ruine*, 183–88; Carole Hillenbrand, *The Crusades: Islamic Perspectives* (Edinburgh, 1999), 593; Siberry, *The New Crusaders*, 68; Treloar, *With the Kaiser*, 27. The wreath was brought to England by T. E. Lawrence and is now in the Imperial War Museum, London.

3. Ende, "Wer ist," 80–81, 84; Hillenbrand, *The Crusades*, 593.

4. Ende, "Wer ist," 84; Hillenbrand, *The Crusades*, 593–94.

5. See Malcolm C. Lyons and David E. P. Jackson, *Saladin: The Politics of the Holy War* (Cambridge, 1982).

6. As a child he had been given Scott's poetry to read. John C. G. Röhl, *Young Wilhelm: The Kaiser's Early Life, 1859–1888* (Cambridge, 1998), 163.

7. For an example of this in a later edition, see Walter Scott, "The Talisman," *Tales of the Crusades* (Dent edition, London and New York, 1899), ix. See Siberry, *The New Crusaders*, 117–18.

8. Ronnie Ellenblum, *Crusader Castles and Modern Histories* (Cambridge, 2007), 9–10.

9. For this and what follows, see Jonathan Riley-Smith, "Islam and the Crusades in History and Imagination, 8 November 1898–11 September 2001," *Crusades* 2 (2003): 151–67. See also Edward Peters, "The *Firanj* are coming—again," *Orbis* 48 (2004): 3–17.

10. Siberry, *The New Crusaders*, 125–28.

11. Norman Daniel, *Islam, Europe, and Empire* (Edinburgh, 1966), 378.

12. Siberry, *The New Crusaders*, 65.

13. Steven Runciman, *A History of the Crusades* (Cambridge, 1951–54), 3:480.

14. *American Historical Review* 60 (1955): 593.

15. Emmanuel Sivan, "Modern Arab Historiography of the Crusades," *Asian and African Studies* 8 (1972): 112; Ende, "Wer ist," 81–82; Peters, "The Firanj," 11. For Abdulhamid and Pan-Islamism, see Jacob M. Landau, *The Politics of Pan-Islamism: Ideology and Organization* (Oxford, 1994), 9–72; Azmi Özcan, *Pan-Islamism: Indian Muslims, the Ottomans and Britain (1877–1924)* (Leiden, 1997), 40–63.

16. See, for example, Amin Malouf, *The Crusades through Arab Eyes*, trans. Jon Rothschild (London, 1984), 266; John L. Esposito, *Unholy War: Terror in the Name of Islam* (Oxford, 2002), 74–75.

17. Michael Brett, "The Near East on the Eve of the Crusades," in *La Primera Cruzada, Novecientos Años después: El Concilio de Clermont y los Orígines del Movimiento Cruzado*, ed. Luis García-Guijarro Ramos (Madrid, 1997), 119–36.

18. Michael A. Köhler, *Allianzen und Verträge zwischen fränkischen und islamischen Herrschern im Vorderen Orient* (Berlin, 1991); Hillenbrand, *The Crusades*, 257–327.

19. Michael Bonner, *Jihad in Islamic History* (Princeton and Oxford, 2006), 137–42.

20. Bonner, *Jihad*, 143–44; Hillenbrand, *The Crusades*, 227–48. Spasms of jihadism were also evident on the Western front, where successive waves of Berber invaders—Almoravids, Almohads, Marinids—brought enthusiasm with them into the Iberian Peninsula.

21. See Osama bin Muhammad bin Laden, *Messages to the World*, ed. Bruce Lawrence, trans. James Howarth (London and New York, 2005), 5, 9, 11, 26, 60–61, 80, 118, 229, 249–50.

22. Hillenbrand, *The Crusades*, 104–8; Emmanuel Sivan, *L'Islam et la croisade*

(Paris, 1968), 29–30; Niall Christie, "Motivating Listeners in the *kitab al-Jihad* of 'Ali ibn Tahir al-Sulami," *Crusades* 6 (2007): 1–14.

23. Alfred Morabia, "Ibn Taymiyya, dernier grand théoricien du Gihad medieval," *Bulletin d'études orientales* 30 (1978), 85–99; Hillenbrand, *The Crusades*, 241–43. See also Alfred Morabia, *Le Gihad dans l'Islam médiéval* (Paris, 1983); Peters, "The *Firanj*," 15–16.

24. For example, see Malcolm C. Lyons, *The Arabian Epic*, (Cambridge, 1995), 1:13–15 (in which Saladin also gets a look-in).

25. Bernard Lewis, *The Muslim Discovery of Europe* (London, 1982), 164–66; Hillenbrand, *The Crusades*, 591.

26. Kamal S. Salibi, *Maronite Historians of Mediaeval Lebanon* (Beirut, 1959).

27. Bernard Lewis, *The Middle East and the West* (London, 1964), 116.

28. Suha Taji-Farouki, "A Case Study in Contemporary Political Islam and the Palestine Question: The Perspective of Hizb al-Tahrir al-Islami," in *Medieval and Modern Perspectives on Muslim-Jewish Relations*, ed. Ronald L. Nettler (*Studies in Muslim-Jewish Relations*, Luxembourg, 1995), 40.

29. *al-hurub as-salibiyya* (singular *al-harb as-salib* is war of the cross; and hence *as-salibiyyun* is crusaders). Sivan, "Modern Arab Historiography," 109–10; Ende, "Wer ist," 80; Hillenbrand, *The Crusades*, 591–92.

30. As, for example, in Syed Ameer Ali's *A Short History of the Saracens*. Peters, "The *Firanj*," 11–12.

31. M. 'A. Matawi in 1954, cited by Sivan, "Modern Arab Historiography," 144; see also 141–48.

32. See Sivan, "Modern Arab Historiography," 128–30.

33. Ende, "Wer ist," 85–86; Hillenbrand, *The Crusades*, 594; Sivan, "Modern Arab Historiography," 112–13.

34. Mahmud Darwish, *Memory for Forgetfulness: August, Beirut, 1982*, trans. Ibrahim Muhawi (Berkeley, 1995), 33–34; Hillenbrand, *The Crusades*, 613.

35. Sivan, "Modern Arab Historiography," 112.

36. Ibid., 119–20. See also Jean Richard, *Histoire des croisades* (Paris, 1996), 488.

37. See Osama bin Muhammad bin Laden, *Messages*, 124.

38. Sivan, "Modern Arab Historiography," 114–18.

39. Ibid., 112.

40. Darwish, *Memory*, 11.

41. Taji-Farouki, "A Case Study," 41. See Hillenbrand, *The Crusades*, 602–9.

42. Sivan, "Modern Arab Historiography," 114, see also 112–13; Ende, "Wer ist," 85–86; Hillenbrand, *The Crusades*, 594.

43. Sivan, "Modern Arab Historiography," 121–25.

44. Although the extent of that influence is debatable. Ibrahim M. Abu-Rabi', *Intellectual Origins of Islamic Resurgence in the Modern Arab World* (Albany, 1996), 139; Gilles Kepel, *Jihad: The Trail of Political Islam*, trans. Anthony F. Roberts (London, 2002), 24–27.

45. Abu-Rabi', *Intellectual Origins*, 205, see also 134–35, 189–206; Ahmad S. Moussalli, *Radical Islamic Fundamentalism: The Ideological and Political Discourse of Sayyid Qutb* (Beirut, 1992); Malise Ruthven, *A Fury for God: The Islamist Attack on America* (London, 2002), 72–98.

46. Sylvia G. Haim, "Sayyid Qutb," *Asian and African Studies* 16 (1982): 154.

47. See Muhammad Farag, quoted in Esposito, *Unholy War*, 63; Hillenbrand, *The Crusades*, 600–2, 609–10; Ilan Pappe, "Understanding the Enemy: A Comparative Analysis of Palestinian Islamist and Nationalist Leaflets, 1920s–1980s," *Studies in Muslim-Jewish Relations: Muslim Jewish Encounters, Intellectual Traditions, and Modern Politics*, ed. Ronald L. Nettler and Suha Taji-Farouki (Amsterdam, 1998), 87–107; Ruthven, *A Fury for God*, 94, 185. For an example of the use of the term *zio-crusaders* for the Israelis, see "Statement," by Ayman az-Zawahiri, http://analysis.threatswatch.org/2006/07/the-zawahiri-proclamation-one, July 27, 2006.

48. Osama bin Muhammad bin Laden, *Messages*, 16.

49. Ibid., 59.

50. Osama bin Muhammad bin Laden, "Statement," www.satp.org/satporgtp/countries/pakistan/document/papers/Transcript_osama.htm, April 2006.

51. Ibid., 108–9.

52. Ibid., April 2006.

53. Ibid., 121, 127–28.

54. See Bonner, *Jihad*, 157–61.

55. Cardinal Walter Kasper, "Address to the Archbishop of Athens," www.vatican.va/roman_curia/pontifical_councils/chrstuni/documents/rc_pc_chrstuni_doc_20030214_kasper-greece_en.html, February 14, 2003.

56. Vatican, "The Day of Pardon, March 12, 2000," www.vatican.va/jubilee_2000/jubilevents/events_day_pardon_en.htm.

57. *The Oxford Dictionary of the Christian Church*, ed. Frank L. Cross and Elizabeth A. Livingstone, 3rd ed. (Oxford, 1997), 969.

58. *The Oxford Dictionary*, 959.

59. Elizabeth Siberry, "Images of the Crusades in the Nineteenth and Twentieth Centuries," in *The Oxford Illustrated History of the Crusades*, ed. Jonathan Riley-Smith (Oxford, 1995), 384–85.

60. Jonathan Riley-Smith, "Revival and Survival," in *The Oxford Illustrated History of the Crusades*, ed. Jonathan Riley-Smith (Oxford, 1995), 386–89.

61. Siberry, *The New Crusaders*, 87.

62. Ibid., 87–88.

63. See Jay M. Winter, *Sites of Memory, Sites of Mourning: The Great War in European Cultural History* (Cambridge, 1998).

64. Siberry, *The New Crusaders*, 103.

65. Ibid., 98–100.

CONCLUSION

1. Humbert of Romans, "Opus tripartitum," in *Fasciculus rerum expetendarum et fugiendarum*, ed. Edward Brown (London, 1690), 193.

BIBLIOGRAPHY

MANUSCRIPT SOURCES

Archivio Generale dei Missionari d'Africa, Rome (A.G.M.Afr.)

Ms. B.16.82 Constitution et Règle de l'Institut des Frères Armés ou Pionniers du Sahara

The Library of the British Association of the Sovereign Military Order of Malta, St John's Wood, London (BASMOM)

Letter Book 1

The Library and Museum of the Most Venerable Order of St John, St John's Gate, London (MVO)

Archives
Copies of Documents
Historical memoranda, vols. 1, 3
Ms K 8/1 Bonds
Ms K 32/4 First, Second and Third Instruments of Convention and Letter of Instruction
OSJ Anglia Minutes
Woof, Richard, *Order of St John of Jerusalem in England* (1872). Proof Copy

Printed Sources

Actes des comtes de Flandre, 1071–1128. Ed. Fernand Vercauteren. Brussels, 1938.

"Administrative Regulations for the Hospital of St. John in Jerusalem dating from the 1180s." Ed. Susan Edgington. *Crusades* 4 (2005).

Albert of Aachen. *Historia Ierosolimitana.* Ed. Susan Edgington. Oxford, 2007.

Alexander III, Pope. "Piam admodum." *Cartulaire général de l'ordre des Hospitaliers.* 1:360–61.

——. "Quam amabilis Deo." *Papsturkunden für Templer und Johanniter.* 2:159–62.

"Annalista Saxo." *MGHS* 6.

The Apostolic See and the Jews: Documents. Ed. Shlomo Simonsohn. 8 vols. Toronto, 1988–91.

Augustine of Hippo. "Contra Faustum Manichaeum." *PL* 42.

——. *De civitate Dei.* Ed. Bernard Dombart and Alphonse Kalb, 2 vols. *CCSL* 47–48. Turnhout, 1955.

——. *Quaestionum in Heptateuchum Libri VII.* Ed. Benedikt Schwank. *CCSL* 33. Turnhout, 1958.

Baldric of Bourgueil. "Historia Jerosolimitana." *RHC Oc* 4.

Bernard of Clairvaux. "De consideratione." Vol. 3, *Sancti Bernardi Opera*, ed. Jean Leclercq et al. Rome, 1957–77.

——. "Epistolae." Vol. 8, *Sancti Bernardi Opera*, ed. Jean Leclercq et al. Rome, 1957–77.

"Bessarions Instruktion für die Kreuzzugspredigt in Venedig (1463)." Ed. Ludwig Mohler. *Römische Quartalschrift* 35 (1927).

Cartulaire général de l'ordre des Hospitaliers de St. Jean de Jérusalem. Ed. Joseph Delaville Le Roulx, 4 vols. Paris, 1894–1906.

Castiglione, Sabba di. *Ricordi a Fra Bartholomeo di Castiglione suo nipote.* Bologna, 1549.

CCCM—Corpus Christianorum. Continuatio Medievalis. Turnhout, 1966.

CCSL—Corpus Christianorum. Series Latina. Turnhout, 1954.

Charles of Anjou. "Déposition." Ed. Paul E. D. Riant. In *Notices et documents publiés pour la société de l'histoire de France à l'occasion du cinquantième anniversaire de sa fondation.* Paris, 1884.

Conciliorum Oecumenicorum Decreta. Ed. Giuseppe Alberigo et al. Freiburg, 1962.

Conder, Claude R. *The Latin Kingdom of Jerusalem, 1099 to 1291 AD.* London, 1897.

Contarini, Gianpietro. *Historia delle cose successe dal principio della guerra mossa da Selim Ottomano a' Venetiani.* Venice, 1572.

Darwish, Mahmoud. *Memory for Forgetfulness: August, Beirut, 1982*. Trans. Ibrahim Muhawi. Berkeley, 1995.

De expugnatione Lyxbonensi. Ed. and trans. Charles W. David. New York, 1936.

Ekkehard of Aura. "Hierosolymita." *RHC Oc* 5.

"The Elstow Sermon." In *The Preaching of the Crusades*, ed. Cole, 232–34.

Eudes of Châteauroux. "Sermo I ad assumendam crucem." In *Crusade Propaganda*, ed. Maier, 128–42.

——. "Sermo II ad invitatione ad crucem." In *Crusade Propaganda*, ed. Maier, 144–50.

——. "Sermo III de invitatione ad crucem." In *Crusade Propaganda*, ed. Maier, 152–58.

——. "Sermo IV de invitatione ad crucem." In *Crusade Propaganda*, ed. Maier, 160–64.

——. "Sermo V ad invitandam ad crucem." In *Crusade Propaganda*, ed. Maier, 166–74.

——. "Sermones in anniversario Roberti comitis Attrabatensis." In *The Preaching of the Crusades*, ed. Cole, 235–43.

Eudes of Deuil. *De Profectione Ludovici VII in Orientem*. Ed. Virginia Berry. New York, 1948.

Gaulis, Georges. *La ruine d'une empire: Abd-ul-Hamid, ses amis et ses peuples*. Paris, 1913.

Gerald of Wales. "Itinerarium Cambriae." In *Opera*, ed. James Francis Dimock. Rolls Series 21/6. London, 1868.

Gilbert of Tournai. "Sermo I ad crucesignatos et crucesignandos." In *Crusade Propaganda*, ed. Maier, 176–90.

——. "Sermo III ad crucesignatos et crucesignandos." In *Crusade Propaganda*, ed. Maier, 198–208.

Gregory VIII, Pope. "Audita tremendi." In "Historia de expeditione Friderici imperatoris," ed. Anton Chroust, *MGH Scriptores rerum Germanicarum*, n.s. 5: 6–10. Berlin, 1928.

Guibert of Nogent. *Dei gesta per Francos*. Ed. Robert B. C. Huygens. CCCM 127A. Turnholt, 1996.

——. *De vita sua*. Ed. Edmond René Labande. Paris, 1981.

Gunther of Pairis. *Hystoria Constantinopolitana*. Ed. Peter Orth. *Spolia Berolinensia* 5. Hildesheim and Zürich, 1994.

Hebräische Berichte über die Judenverfolgungen während des Ersten Kreuzzugs. Ed. Eva Haverkamp. *MGH Hebräische Texte aus dem mittelalterlichen Deutschland* 1. Hanover, 2005.

Helmold of Bosau. "Chronica Slavorum." *MGHS* 21.

Henry of Livonia. *Chronicon Livoniae.* Ed. Leonid Arbusow and Adolf Bauer. *MGH Scriptores rerum Germanicarum,* n.s. 31, 2nd ed. Hanover, 1955.

"Historia de expeditione Friderici imperatoris." Ed. Anton Chroust. *MGH Scriptores rerum Germanicarum,* n.s. 5. Berlin, 1928.

Humbert of Romans. *De predicatione sancte crucis.* Nuremburg, 1490.

———. "Opus tripartitum." In *Fasciculus rerum expetendarum et fugiendarum,* ed. Edward Brown. London, 1690.

———. "Sermo I ad peregrinos crucesignatos." In *Crusade Propaganda,* ed. Maier, 210–14.

Ibn Shaddad. *The Rare and Excellent History of Saladin.* Trans. Donald Sidney Richards. Aldershot, 2001.

Innocent III, Pope. "Experimento didicimus." *PL* 215:1339–41.

———. "Gaudemus in Domino." *PL* 216:906–7.

———. "Licet circa statutum." In *Innocent III, Die Register,* ed. Othmar Hageneder et al., 1:807–9. Graz, Cologne, Rome, and Vienna, 1964–.

———. "Protector in se." *PL* 216:703–4.

———. "Quia maior." In *Studien zum Register Innocenz III,* ed. Georgine Tangl, 88–97. Weimar, 1929.

James of Vitry. *Lettres.* Ed. Robert B.C. Huygens. Leiden, 1960.

———. "Sermo ad fratres ordinis militaris." In *Analecta novissima,* ed. Jean Baptiste Pitra, 2:414–21. Paris, 1888.

———. "Sermo I ad crucesignatos vel–signandos." In *Crusade Propaganda,* ed. Maier, 82–98.

———. "Sermo II ad crucesignatos vel–signandos." In *Crusade Propaganda,* ed. Maier, 100–26.

John of Abbeville. "Sermo ad crucesignatos." In *The Preaching of the Crusades,* ed. Cole, 222–26.

John of Mantua. "Tractatus in Cantica Canticorum." In *Ioannis Mantuani in Cantica Canticorum et De Sancta Maria Tractatus ad Comitissam Matildam,* ed. Bernhard Bischoff and Burkhard Taeger. Freiburg, 1973.

John of Joinville. *Vie de Saint Louis.* Ed. Jacques Montfrin. Paris, 1995.

Die Kreuzzugsbriefe aus den Jahren, 1088–1100. Ed. Heinrich Hagenmeyer. Innsbruck, 1901.

Landulf the Younger. "Historia Mediolanensis." *MGHS* 20.

Leo XIII, Pope. "Inclytam antiquitate originis." In *Histoire Politique,* ed. Pierredon, 3:269–72.

———. "Solemne semper." In *Histoire Politique,* ed. Pierredon, 3:260–64.

"Liber memorabilium rerum seu etiam cartarum abbatiae Besensis." In Vol. 1, *Spicilegium sive collectio veterum aliquot scriptorum.* Ed. Luc d'Achéry. Paris, 1655–77.

Louis IX of France. "Epistola." In Vol. 5, *Historiae Francorum Scriptores*. Ed. François Du Chesne. Paris, 1636–49.

Matthew Paris. *Chronica maiora*. Ed. Henry Richards Luard. 7 vols. Rolls Series 57. London, 1872–83.

MGH—Monumenta Germaniae Historica.

MGHS—MGH Scriptores in Folio et Quarto. Ed. Georg H. Pertz et al. 38 vols. Hanover and Leipzig, 1826.

Michaud, Joseph-François. *Histoire des croisades*. 4th ed. 6 vols. Paris, 1825–29.

Napoleon I. *Mémoires et Oeuvres*. Ed. Tancrède Martel. Paris, 1910.

Oliver of Paderborn. *Schriften*. Ed. Hermann Hoogeweg. Tübingen, 1894.

Orderic Vitalis. *Historia aecclesiastica*. Ed. and trans. Marjorie Chibnall. 6 vols. Oxford, 1969–79.

Osama bin Muhammad bin Laden. *Messages to the World*. Ed. Bruce Lawrence, trans. James Howarth. London and New York, 2005.

Papsturkunden für Templer und Johanniter. Ed. Rudolf Hiestand (*Vorarbeiten zum Oriens Pontificius I–II*). 2 vols. Göttingen, 1972–84.

Peter of Vaux-de-Cernay. *Hystoria Albigensis*. Ed. Pascal Guébin and Ernest Lyon. 3 vols. Paris, 1926.

Peter the Venerable. *The Letters*. Ed. Giles Constable. 2 vols. Cambridge, MA, 1967.

PL—Patrologiae Cursus Completus. Series Latina. Comp. Jacques Paul Migne. 217 vols. and 4 vols. of indexes. Paris, 1841–64.

Le procès des Templiers. Ed. Jules Michelet. 2 vols. Paris, 1841–51.

RHC—Recueil des historians des croisades. Ed. Académie des Inscriptions et Belles Lettres. Paris, 1841–1906.

RHC Oc—RHC Historiens occidentaux. 5 vols. Paris, 1844–95.

RHGF—Recueil des historiens des Gaules et de la France. Ed. Martin Bouquet et al. 24 vols. Paris, 1737–1904.

Richard of Poitiers. "Chronicon." *RHGF* 12.

Robert of Rheims. "Historia Iherosolimitana." *RHC Oc* 3.

Roger of Salisbury. "Sermo ad crucesignatos." In *The Preaching of the Crusades*, ed. Cole, 227–31.

Saint-Denis de Nogent-le-Rotrou, 1031–1789, Histoire et cartulaire. Ed. Hector J. H. J. G. de Souancé and Charles Metais. Vannes, 1899.

Scott, Walter. "The Talisman." In *Tales of the Crusaders*. 4 vols. Edinburgh, 1825; Dent edition: London and New York, 1899.

Sigebert of Gembloux. "Leodicensium epistola adversus Paschalem Papam." *MGH Libelli de Lite Imperatorum et Pontificum* 2.

Thomas Aquinas. *Quaestiones Quodlibetales*. Ed. Raimundo Spiazzi. Turin, 1956.

———. *Summa Theologica*. Ed. Altera Romana. 5 vols. Rome, 1894.

The Times. November 1, 10, and 16, 1898. London.

Treloar, William, *With the Kaiser in the East, 1898*. London, 1915.

"A Twelfth-Century Description of the Jerusalem Hospital." Ed. Benjamin Z. Kedar. In *The Military Orders: Volume 2*, ed. Helen Nicholson. Aldershot, 1998.

Vetera monumenta historica Hungariam sacram illustrantia. Ed. Augustin Theiner. 2 vols. Rome, 1859–60.

Wenrich of Trier. "Epistola sub Theoderici episcopi Virdunensis nomine composite." *MGH Libelli de Lite Imperatorum et Pontificum* 1.

INTERNET MATERIAL

Ayman az-Zawahiri. "Statement." http://analysis.threatswatch.org/2006/07/the-zawahiri-proclamation-one. July 27, 2006.

Kasper, Cardinal Walter. "Address to the Archbishop of Athens." www.vatican.va/roman_curia/pontifical_councils/chrstuni/documents/rc_pc_chrstuni_doc_20030214_kasper-greece_en.html. February 14, 2003.

Osama bin Muhammad bin Laden. "Statement." www.satp.org/satporgtp/countries/pakistan/document/papers/Transcript_osama.htm. April 2006.

Vatican. "The Day of Pardon, March 12, 2000." www. vatican.va/jubilee_2000/jubilevents/events_day_pardon_en.htm.

Williams, Rowan, archbishop of Canterbury. "What is Christianity?" Lecture given at the International Islamic University in Islamabad, Pakistan, November 23, 2005. www.archbishopofcanterbury.org/sermons_speeches/2005/051123.htm

SECONDARY WORKS

Abulafia, David. "Invented Italians in the Courtois Charters." In *Crusade and Settlement*, ed. Peter W. Edbury. Cardiff, 1985.

Abu-Rabi', Ibrahim M. *Intellectual Origins of Islamic Resurgence in the Modern Arab World*. Albany, 1996.

Acton, Harold M. *The Bourbons of Naples (1734–1825)*. London, 1974.

Adão Fonseca, Luis. "As Ordens Militares e a Expansão." *A Alta Nobreza e a Fundação do Estado da Índia*. Lisbon, 2004.

———. "La storiografia dell'espansione marittima portoghese (secc. XIV-XV)." *Bullettino dell'Istituto Storico Italiano per il Medio Evo* 106 (2004).

Adas, Michael. *Prophets of Rebellion*. Cambridge, 1979.

Anderson, Matthew Smith. *The Eastern Question, 1774–1923*. London, 1966.

Anstruther, Ian. *The Knight and the Umbrella*. London, 1963.

Argenti, Philip. *The Occupation of Chios by the Genoese and their Administration of the Island, 1346–1566*. 3 vols. Cambridge, 1958.

Arnold, Udo. "Eight Hundred Years of the Teutonic Order." In *The Military Orders: Fighting for the Faith and Caring for the Sick*, ed. Malcolm Barber. Aldershot, 1994.

Becker, Alfons. *Papst Urban II (1088–1099)*. 2 vols. Stuttgart, 1964–88.

Bonner, Michael. *Jihad in Islamic History*. Princeton and Oxford, 2006.

Brett, Michael. "The Near East on the Eve of the Crusades." In *La Primera Cruzada, Novecientos Años después: El Concilio de Clermont y los Orígines del Movimiento Cruzado*, ed. Luis García-Guijarro Ramos. Madrid, 1997.

Bronisch, Alexander P. *Reconquista und heiliger Krieg: Die Deutung des Krieges im christlichen Spanien von den Westgoten bis ins frühe 12. Jahrhundert*. Münster, 1998.

Brundage, James. *Medieval Canon Law and the Crusader*. Madison, 1969.

Bull, Marcus. *Knightly Piety and the Lay Response to the First Crusade: The Limousin and Gascony, c. 970–c. 1130*. Oxford, 1993.

——. "Views of Muslims and of Jerusalem in Miracle Stories, c. 1000–c. 1200: Reflections on the Study of First Crusaders' Motivations." In *The Experience of Crusading: Volume One*, ed. Marcus Bull and Norman Housley. Cambridge, 2003.

The Cambridge Economic History of Europe, vol. 1. Ed. John H. Clapham. Cambridge, 1941.

Carey, Peter. "The Origins of the Java War (1825–30)." *English Historical Review* 91 (1976).

Chazan, Robert. *European Jewry and the First Crusade*. Berkeley, 1987.

——. *Medieval Stereotypes and Modern Antisemitism*. Berkeley, 1997.

Chevedden, Paul. "Canon 2 of the Council of Clermont (1095) and the Crusade Indulgence." *Annuarium Historiae Conciliorum* 37 (2005).

Christie, Niall. "Motivating Listeners in the *kitab al-Jihad* of 'Ali ibn Tahir al-Sulami." *Crusades* 6 (2007).

Cohen, Jeremy. *Sanctifying the Name of God: Jewish Martyrs and Jewish Memories of the First Crusade*. Philadelphia, 2004.

Cole, Penny J. *The Preaching of the Crusades to the Holy Land, 1095–1270*. Cambridge, MA, 1991.

Cole-Mackintosh, Ronnie. *A Century of Service to Mankind*. London, 1986.

Constable, Giles. "The Place of the Crusader in Medieval Society." *Viator* 29 (1998).

——. "The Historiography of the Crusades." In *The Crusades from the Perspective* of *Byzantium and the Muslim World*, ed. Angeliki E. Laiou and Roy P. Motta-hedeh. Washington, DC, 2001.

Constans, Claire and Philippe Lamarque. *Les Salles des Croisades: Château de Versailles*. Versailles, 2002.

Cowdrey, H. E. John. "Christianity and the Morality of Warfare During the First Century of Crusading." In *The Experience of Crusading, Volume One: Western Approaches*. Ed. Marcus Bull and Norman Housley. Cambridge, 2003.

Daniel, Norman. *Islam, Europe, and Empire*. Edinburgh, 1966.

Dickson, Gary. *The Children's Crusade*. Basingstoke, 2008.

Diderot, Denis, and Jean Le Rond d'Alembert. *Encyclopédie*. 17 vols. Paris, 1751–65.

Driault, Edouard, and Michel Lhéritier. *Histoire diplomatique de la Grèce de 1821 à nos jours*. 5 vols. Paris, 1925–26.

Duchhardt, Heinz. "La guerre et le droit des gens dans l'Europe du XVIe au XVIIIe siècle." In *Guerre et concurrence entre les Etats européens du XIVe au XVIIIe siècle*, ed. Philippe Contamine. Paris, 1998.

Ellenblum, Ronnie. *Frankish Rural Settlement in the Latin kingdom of Jerusalem*. Cambridge, 1998.

——. *Crusader Castles and Modern Histories*. Cambridge, 2007.

Ende, Werner. "Wer ist ein Glaubensheld, wer ist ein Ketzer." *Die Welt des Islams* NS 23 (1984).

Esposito, John L. *Unholy War. Terror in the Name of Islam*. Oxford, 2002.

Flori, Jean. *L'Essor de Chevalerie XIe-XIIe siècles*. Geneva, 1986.

Folda, Jaroslav. *Crusader Art in the Holy Land from the Third Crusade to the Fall of Acre, 1187–1291*. Cambridge, 2005.

Fonnesberg-Schmidt, Iben. *The Popes and the Baltic Crusades, 1147–1254*. Leiden, 2007.

Garcez Teixeira, Francisco Augusto. *Tomar*. Porto, 1929.

Grousset, René. *Histoire des croisades*. 3 vols. Paris, 1934–36.

Haim, Sylvia G. "Sayyid Qutb." *Asian and African Studies* 16 (1982).

Helgeland, John. "The Early Church and War: The Sociology of Idolatry." In *Peace in a Nuclear Age*, ed. Charles J. Reid. Washington, DC, 1986.

Hillenbrand, Carole. *The Crusades: Islamic Perspectives*. Edinburgh, 1999.

Housley, Norman. *The Italian Crusades*. Oxford, 1982.

——. *The Later Crusades, 1274–1580*. Oxford, 1992.

——. *Documents on the Later Crusades, 1274–1580*. Basingstoke, 1996.

——. *Religious Warfare in Europe, 1400–1536*. Oxford, 2002.

——. *Contesting the Crusades*. Oxford, 2006.

Jordan, William C. *Louis IX and the Challenge of the Crusade*. Princeton, 1979.

Kedar, Benjamin Z. *Crusade and Mission: European Approaches toward the Muslims*. Princeton, 1984.

Keegan, John. *The Face of Battle*. London, 1976.

Keen, Maurice. *Chivalry*. New Haven and London, 1984.

Kenaan-Kedar, Nurith, and Benjamin Z. Kedar. "The Significance of a Twelfth-Century Sculptural Group: Le Retour du Croisé." In *Dei gesta per Francos*, ed. Michel Balard, Benjamin Z. Kedar, and Jonathan Riley-Smith. Aldershot, 2001.

Kepel, Gilles. *Jihad: The Trail of Political Islam*. Trans. Anthony F. Roberts. London, 2002.

Knobler, Adam. "Saint Louis and French Political Culture." In *Medievalism in Europe II: Studies in Medievalism*, ed. Leslie J. Workman and Kathleen Verduin. Cambridge, 1996.

Köhler, Michael A. *Allianzen und Verträge zwischen fränkischen und islamischen Herrschern im Vorderen Orient*. Berlin, 1991.

Krey, August. "Review of Steven Runciman, *A History of the Crusades*." *American Historical Review* 60 (1955).

Landau, Jacob M. *The Politics of Pan-Islamism: Ideology and Organization*. Oxford, 1994.

Lewis, Bernard. *The Middle East and the West*. London, 1964.

——. *The Muslim Discovery of Europe*. London, 1982.

Licence, Tom. "The Templars and the Hospitallers, Christ and the Saints." *Crusades* 4 (2005).

——. "The Military Orders as Monastic Orders." *Crusades* 5 (2006).

Linder, Amnon. *Raising Arms: Liturgy in the Struggle to Liberate Jerusalem in the Late Middle Ages*. Turnhout, 2003.

Lloyd, Simon. *English Society and the Crusade, 1216–1307*. Oxford, 1988.

Longnon, Jean. *Les français d'Outremer au moyen-âge*. Paris, 1929.

Lunt, William E. *Papal Revenues in the Middle Ages*. 2 vols. New York, 1934.

——. *Financial Relations of the Papacy with England*. 2 vols. Cambridge, MA, 1939–62.

Luttrell, Anthony. "The Spiritual Life of the Hospitallers of Rhodes." In *Die Spiritualität der Ritterorden im Mittelater*, ed. Zeon Hubert Nowak, 75–96. Toruń, 1993. Reprinted in Anthony T. Luttrell, *The Hospitaller State on Rhodes and Its Western Provinces, 1306–1462*. Aldershot, 1999.

Lyons, Malcolm C. *The Arabian Epic*. 3 vols. Cambridge, 1995.

Lyons, Malcolm C., and David E. P. Jackson. *Saladin: The Politics of the Holy War*. Cambridge, 1982.

Maccarone, Michele. *Vicarius Christi: Storia del titole papale*. Rome, 1952.

——. "Orvieto e la predicazione della crociata." *Studi su Innocenzo III. Italia sacra* 17. Padua, 1972.

MacDonogh, Giles. *The Last Kaiser: William the Impetuous.* London, 2000.

Maier, Christoph T. *Preaching the Crusades: Mendicant Friars and the Cross in the Thirteenth Century.* Cambridge, 1994.

——. "Crusade and Rhetoric against the Muslim Colony of Lucera: Eudes of Châteauroux's *Sermones de Rebellione Sarracenorum Lucherie in Apulia.*" *Journal of Medieval History* 21 (1995).

——. "Crisis, Liturgy, and the Crusade in the Twelfth and Thirteenth Centuries." *Journal of Ecclesiastical History* 48 (1997).

——. *Crusade Propaganda and Ideology.* Cambridge, 2000.

Malouf, Amin. *The Crusades through Arab Eyes.* Trans. Jon Rothschild. London, 1984.

Morabia, Alfred. "Ibn Taymiyya, dernier grand théoricien du Gihad medieval." *Bulletin d'études orientales* 30 (1978).

——. *Le Gihad dans l'Islam médiéval.* Paris, 1983.

Moussalli, Ahmad S. *Radical Islamic Fundamentalism: The Ideological and Political Discourse of Sayyid Qutb.* Beirut, 1992.

Muldoon, James. *Popes, Lawyers, and Infidels.* Liverpool, 1979.

Munholland, Kim. "Michaud's *History of the Crusades* and the French Crusade in Algeria under Louis Philippe." In *The Popularization of Images*, ed. Petra ten-Doesschate Chu and Gabriel P. Weisberg. Princeton, 1994.

Munro, Dane. *Memento Mori.* 2 vols. Valletta, 2005.

The Oxford Dictionary of the Christian Church. Ed. Frank L. Cross and Elizabeth A. Livingstone. 3rd ed. Oxford, 1997.

Oxford Dictionary of National Biography. Ed. Henry C. G. Matthews and Brian Harrison, 61 vols. (Oxford, 2004).

Özcan, Azmi. *Pan-Islamism: Indian Muslims, the Ottomans, and Britain (1877–1924).* Leiden, 1997.

Pakenham, Thomas. *The Scramble for Africa, 1876–1912.* London, 1991.

Palmer, Alan. *The Kaiser: Warlord of the Second Reich.* London, 1978.

Pappe, Ilan. "Understanding the Enemy: A Comparative Analysis of Palestinian Islamist and Nationalist Leaflets, 1920s-1980s." In *Studies in Muslim-Jewish Relations: Muslim Jewish Encounters, Intellectual Traditions, and Modern Politics*, ed. Ronald L. Nettler and Suha Taji-Farouki. Amsterdam, 1998.

Paravicini, Werner. *Die Preussenreise des Europäischen Adels.* 2 vols. Sigmaringen, 1989–95.

Peters, Edward. "The *Firanj* are coming—again." *Orbis* 48 (2004).

Phillips, Jonathan. "St. Bernard of Clairvaux: The Low Countries and the Lisbon Letter of the Second Crusade." *Journal of Ecclesiastical History* 48 (1997).

Pierredon, Michel de. *Histoire Politique de l'Ordre Souverain de Saint-Jean de Jérusalem (Ordre de Malte) de 1789 à 1955.* 2nd ed. 6 vols. Paris, 1990–2000.

Piro, Nicholas de. *The Temple of the Knights of Malta.* Sliema, 1999.

Postan, Michael M. "The Trade of Medieval Europe: The North." *The Cambridge Economic History of Europe*, vol. 2. 2nd ed. Cambridge, 1987.

Powell, James. *Anatomy of a Crusade, 1213–1221.* Philadelphia, 1986.

Pringle, Denys. *The Churches of the Crusader Kingdom of Jerusalem: A Corpus.* 3 vols. Cambridge, 1993–.

Renault, François. *Lavigerie, l'Esclavage Africain et l'Europe, 1868–92.* 2 vols. Paris, 1971.

——. *Cardinal Lavigerie: Churchman, Prophet, and Missionary.* Trans. John O'Donohue. London, 1994.

Richard, Jean. *Saint Louis.* Paris, 1983.

——. *Histoire des croisades.* Paris, 1996.

Riley-Smith, Jonathan. *The Knights of St. John in Jerusalem and Cyprus, c. 1050–1310.* London, 1967.

——. "Crusading as an Act of Love." *History* 65 (1980).

——. *The First Crusade and the Idea of Crusading.* London, 1986.

——, ed. *The Atlas of the Crusades.* London, 1991.

——. "The Order of St. John in England, 1827–1858." In *The Military Orders: Fighting for the Faith and Caring for the Sick*, ed. Malcolm Barber. Aldershot, 1994.

——, ed. *The Oxford Illustrated History of the Crusades.* Oxford, 1995.

——. "Revival and Survival." In *The Oxford Illustrated History of the Crusades*, ed. Jonathan Riley-Smith. Oxford, 1995.

——. *The First Crusaders, 1095–1131.* Cambridge, 1997.

——. "Casualties and the Number of Knights on the First Crusade." *Crusades* 1 (2002).

——. "Christian Violence and the Crusades." In *Religious Violence between Christians and Jews*, ed. Anna Sapir Abulafia. Basingstoke, 2002.

——. *What Were the Crusades?* 3rd ed. Basingstoke, 2002.

——. "Islam and the Crusades in History and Imagination, 8 November 1898–11 September 2001." *Crusades* 2 (2003).

——. *The Crusades: A History.* 2nd ed. London, 2005.

Röhl, John C. G. *Young Wilhelm: The Kaiser's Early Life, 1859–1888.* Cambridge, 1998.

Rousset, Paul. "Un Huguenot propose une croisade: Le projet de François de la Noue (1580–1585)." *Zeitschrift für Schweizerische Kirchengeschichte (Revue d'histoire ecclésiastique suisse)* 72 (1978).

Runciman, Steven. *A History of the Crusades.* 3 vols. Cambridge, 1951–54.

Russell, Frederick H. *The Just War in the Middle Ages.* Cambridge, 1975.

Ruthven, Malise. *A Fury for God: The Islamist Attack on America.* London, 2002.

Salibi, Kamal S. *Maronite Historians of Mediaeval Lebanon.* Beirut, 1959.

Schwenk, Bernd. *Calatrava: Entstehung und Frühgeschichte eines Spanischen Ritterordens Zisterziensischer Observanz im 12. Jahrhundert.* Münster, 1992.

Scicluna, Hannibal P. *The Church of St. John in Valletta.* San Martin, 1955.

Setton, Kenneth M. *The Papacy and the Levant (1204–1571).* 4 vols. Philadelphia, 1976–84.

——. *Venice, Austria, and the Turks in the Seventeenth Century.* Philadelphia, 1991.

Siberry, Elizabeth. *Criticism of Crusading, 1095–1274.* Oxford, 1985.

——. "Images of the Crusades in the Nineteenth and Twentieth Centuries." In *The Oxford Illustrated History of the Crusades,* ed. Riley-Smith. Oxford, 1995.

——. *The New Crusaders: Images of the Crusades in the Nineteenth and Early Twentieth Centuries.* Aldershot, 2000.

Silva, Isabel Morgado S. E., and Pimenta, Maria Cristina. "As Ordens de Santiago e de Cristo e a Fundação do Estado da Índia: Uma Perspectiva de Estudo." *A Alta Nobreza e a Fundação do Estado da Índia.* Lisbon, 2004.

Sire, Henry J.A. *The Knights of Malta.* New Haven and London, 1994.

Sivan, Emmanuel. *L'Islam et la croisade.* Paris, 1968.

——. "Modern Arab Historiography of the Crusades." *Asian and African Studies* 8 (1972).

Smith, Caroline. *Crusading in the Age of Joinville.* Aldershot, 2006.

Tai, Hue-Tam Ho. *Millenarianism and Peasant Politics in Vietnam.* Cambridge, MA, 1983.

Taji-Farouki, Suha. "A Case Study in Contemporary Political Islam and the Palestine Question: The Perspective of Hizb al-Tahrir al-Islami." In *Medieval and Modern Perspectives on Muslim-Jewish Relations,* ed. Ronald L. Nettler. *Studies in Muslim-Jewish Relations,* Luxembourg, 1995.

Thiriet, Freddy. *La Romanie Vénitienne au Moyen Age.* Paris, 1959.

Thompson, James W. *An Economic and Social History of the Middle Ages (300–1300).* New York, 1928.

Twickel, Maximilian von. "Die nationalen Assoziationen des Malteserordens in Deutschland." In *Der Johanniterorden, Der Malteserorden,* ed. Adam Wienand. Cologne, 1970.

Tyerman, Christopher. *England and the Crusades.* Chicago and London, 1988.

——. *Fighting for Christendom: Holy War and the Crusades* (Oxford, 2004)

——. *God's War: A New History of the Crusades.* London, 2006.

Watson, Peter. *War on the Mind: The Military Uses and Abuses of Psychology.* London, 1978.

Winter, Jay M. *Sites of Memory, Sites of Mourning: The Great War in European Cultural History.* Cambridge, 1998.

INDEX

Abbreviations: ab = abbot; archbp = archbishop; b = bishop; c = count; d = duke; e = emperor; gm = grand master; k = king; ka = kaiser; kdom = kingdom; l = lord; p = pope; pl = papal legate; s = sultan; st = saint

the Redeemer, 63; Dormition abbey, 63–64; German hospice, 64; Holy Sepulchre, 16, 20, 37, 41, 63; Mount of Olives, 64; Mount Sion, 63; St Anne, 46

Jerusalem, heavenly, 32

Jerusalem, kdom, 3–4, 42, 60, 73

Jerusalem, Latin patriarchate, 46

Jews, 1, 3–4, 26–27, 70, 72; persecution of 3–4, 26–27

jihads, jihadis, 6, 25, 69–70, 72–76, 78

Joan of Arc, st, 78

John of Abbeville, 16, 39

John the Baptist, st, 11

John of Capistrano, st, 5

John of Ibelin, c Jaffa, 20

John, l Joinville, 30, 34

John Paul II, p, 4, 77

Joseph of Arimathea, st, 32

just cause, 11–12, 14–17

just persecution, 13

just war theory, modern, 13–14

Kashmir, 75

Kemal, Namik, 64

Kerr, Alfred, 63

The Kingdom of Heaven, 67

Kipchak Turks, 69

Knights Hospitaller, 1, 10, 21–23, 35–36, 43–44, 47–58, 61, 63, 77; French capitular commission, 54–56; lieutenant grand masters, 54–58

Knights Templar, 10, 22, 67, 90

Königsberg, 35

Krey, August, 66

Kurds, 64

Lachelin, Joseph, 94

laity, 2, 5–6, 9–10, 33, 35–36, 41, 43

La Noue, Francis of, 5

Las Navas de Tolosa, battle of, 24

Lateran Council, Fourth, 5

Lavigerie, Cardinal Charles-Martial Allemand-, archbp Algiers, 45–52, 59, 61, 68, 77, 93

League of Nations, 60

Lebanon, 46, 59–60, 71–72

legitimate authority, 12, 14–15, 17–19

Leo XIII, p, 47–48, 52, 77

Leopold VI, d Austria, 20

Leopold II, k Belgium, 49

Lepanto, battle of, 3, 24, 34

lepers, 34

Le Puy, 37

Lessing, Gotthold Ephraim, 65; *Nathan the Wise,* 65

Letter of Instruction, 57

Levant, 46, 56, 59, 70–72; crusades in, 1, 9, 15–18, 26, 30, 42–43, 61; Levant Company, 57; western settlements in, 42, 64, 67, 69–71; *see also* Jerusalem, kdom

liberal democracy, 80

liberal economic historians, 60–61, 72

Lithuania, 9, 16, 35

liturgy, 32, 34–38

Loire, 37

London, 55, 78; Prince's Hall, Piccadilly, 49

Lorraine, 30

Louis VII, k France, 30, 34, 37

Louis IX, st, k France, 5, 20, 30–31, 34, 59, 75

Louis Philippe, k France, 54, 59

love and crusading, 21–23, 32, 40–41; *see also* violence

Luther, Martin, 5